How to Peacefully Overthrow the U.S. Government

A Nonviolent Plan to Reclaim Democracy

JAMES ERGLE

Copyright © 2025 by James Ergle

All rights reserved.

No part of this publication may be reproduced, distributed, or transmitted in any form or by any means, including photocopying, recording, or other electronic or mechanical methods, without the prior written permission of the author, except in the case of brief quotations used in critical reviews, commentary, or educational use.

This book is independently published by the author.

Printed and distributed via IngramSpark (paperback and hardcover).

Ebook edition available through Amazon Kindle.

Cover design and interior layout by the author.

For more work by the author, visit: https://radicalleanings.substack.com

First edition: 2025

ISBN: 979-8-9989896-0-5

For entertainment purposes only

(And also revolution)

James Ergle

"This book advocates only peaceful, legal, and nonviolent methods for structural reform, consistent with the U.S. Constitution and international human rights standards."

Table of Contents

Introduction: What This Book Is—and What It Isn't........................1
Paper Shields: Constitutional Myths and the Rights We Think We Have..3
How the Courts Took Power They Were Never Meant to Hold........8
How the Two Parties Took Control—and How They Stay There...17
How the Wealthy Cut Their Taxes and Made Sure It Stayed That Way...27
Rigged from the Start: Why Our Elections Don't Represent Us— And How to Fix Them..33
Why Don't Americans Vote? And What We Can Do About It........40
Who Exactly IS the Deep State Again?..48
Tools or Tyrants?..55
Artificial Influence: How Corporate Personhood Distorted Democracy...61
Faith and the Flag: The Political Capture of Religion in the U.S....69
Rewriting the Rules: Legal Reforms That Could Shift American Power...77
Narrative Control: How Media Consolidation, Social Platforms, and Think Tanks Shrink the Boundaries of American Politics........86
The Rise and Fall of the Fairness Doctrine — and Why Rebuilding It Today Would Almost Certainly Fail..94
Who Gets to Speak?...103
When the Truth Stopped Mattering: How Free Societies and Dictatorships Both Killed Their Own Media..................................110
Protests Don't Work, Except When They Do.................................141
Born Logged In: How a Hyperconnected Generation Is Rewriting the Political Script..145
The Quiet Coup: How Capital Beat Labor, One Law at a Time...152
The Populist Near-Revolution...162
Why Third Parties Fail—and What It Would Take to Break the Two-Party Lock...170
How a Velvet Revolution Could Happen in America.....................177
How Velvet Revolutions Work...184
What Happens When Reform Fails..192
A Global Proof of Concept...201
The Distance Between Us..210

Closing the Gap..216
The Walls in Our Heads..224
Deadlocked: Why Changing the Constitution Feels Impossible—
And What We Can Do About It..229
Countries and Civilizations That Have Lasted Longer Than the
United States...234
"Too Big to Fail": A Repeating Illusion in World History............243
The Next Uprising Will Clock In: How to Reclaim Power One
Union at a Time...249
Who's Even in Charge Here?..256
Epilogue: If You're Reading This, Things Went to Hell.................264
Sources...273
About the Author...276

Introduction: What This Book Is—and What It Isn't

This is not a manifesto. It is not a call to burn anything down. It's not a theory, a conspiracy, or a protest diary. It's a guide for what to do when everything else has already failed.

The chapters ahead were written over months of obsessive study, political burnout, and a slow, brutal realization: most people aren't disengaged because they're lazy. They're disengaged because the system trained them to be. We were taught to participate just enough to keep the illusion alive—vote every few years, argue on social media, maybe hold a sign—and then get back to work.

But when every vote feels like damage control, when every reform effort dies in committee, and when both parties offer the same donors in different suits, it's not apathy. It's recognition. People know something's wrong. What they don't know is how deep it goes—or how to fight back without getting crushed.

This book is for them.

What you'll find here isn't a silver bullet. There are no perfect systems. What you'll find instead is a map: of the rigged structures, the dead ends, the illusions of choice. And then, once the map is clear, a set of real tools—legal, strategic, and repeatable

—that don't rely on charismatic leaders or viral moments.

These chapters aren't just arguments. They're instructions. They're history, stripped of nostalgia. They're policy, stripped of jargon. They're pressure points, laid bare for anyone willing to push.

There is no single party to blame. The rot is structural. It's reinforced by media systems designed to distract you, by legal systems designed to outlast you, and by cultural myths designed to pacify you. Fixing it will take more than awareness. It will take coordination, discipline, and a willingness to act outside the boundaries of performative politics.

This book will not flatter you. It assumes you're smart. It assumes you're angry. And it assumes that if you're still reading, you're done pretending that the next election will solve it all.

It won't.

But there's still time to do something that might.

Paper Shields: Constitutional Myths and the Rights We Think We Have

The most dangerous obstacles to reform aren't in the law—they're in our heads.

I. The Constitution Guarantees All Rights Forever

Many Americans believe their rights are fixed, permanent, and protected by the Constitution. In reality, nearly every right we think we have exists in flux.

Take privacy. A 2021 Annenberg survey found 65% of Americans wrongly believe the Constitution explicitly guarantees it. But that right is based on judicial interpretation—not textual language—which means it shifts as courts change. Abortion access, LGBTQ+ protections, and digital surveillance all hinge on this fragile foundation.

Some believe locking rights into the Constitution protects against uncertainty. But interpretation shapes reality more than parchment does—as shifting privacy rulings in just the last decade have made clear.

Due process offers no more stability. Police can seize property through civil asset forfeiture without charging anyone with a crime, and courts routinely uphold this. Each year, about $3 billion in assets are taken this way.

II. The Framers Intended One Clear Interpretation

Originalists argue that the Constitution must be understood as it was at the time of ratification. It's a tempting idea—offering stability in an unstable world—but the record doesn't support it.

The Framers were politicians, not prophets. They wrote in deliberately vague terms because they couldn't agree on the hard edges of power or rights. Concepts like "equal protection" and "due process" were meant to evolve.

Originalists say a fixed meaning avoids judicial overreach. But rigidity doesn't ensure justice. In 1789, the Constitution allowed slavery and excluded women from civic life. Progress—racial equality, reproductive rights, labor protections—has come not from freezing the text but by stretching its principles.

III. The Constitution Equally Protects Everyone

In theory, constitutional rights apply to all. In practice, access depends on wealth, location, and status.

Voting rights offer a clear example. Gerrymandered districts dilute representation, and voter ID laws disproportionately impact the poor and nonwhite communities. Yet courts routinely uphold these tactics under the current equal protection framework.

Due process is similarly uneven. Overburdened public defenders handle hundreds of cases at once. And in the criminal system, 95% of convictions come through plea deals—many coerced under threat of harsher penalties. This isn't equal justice; it's triage.

IV. Free Speech, Religion, and Due Process—Misunderstood

Free speech doesn't mean immunity from consequence. It means the government can't punish you for your views. You can still be fired, de-platformed, or criticized. Some see platform bans as censorship—but free speech protects against state suppression, not private limits.

The myth that all viewpoints must be "balanced" in public life fuels divisive rhetoric. A 2022 Gallup poll found that 70% of Americans believe systemic criticism is unpatriotic. In 2023, that belief helped fuel attacks on protestors opposing book bans, amplified by "free speech" language on X.

Religious liberty is misunderstood in the same way. The Constitution prohibits the establishment of religion by the state—but recent rulings have granted religious exemptions that allow employers to deny healthcare coverage or services to others. In *Burwell v. Hobby Lobby* (2014), the Court upheld such an exemption, blurring the line between private belief and public obligation.

V. Why It Matters—and How to Fix It

These myths aren't harmless. They give cover to inequality and elite manipulation. If people believe their rights are guaranteed by paper alone, they stop fighting for real protections. If criticism is labeled "anti-American," then reform becomes treason.

In 2023, X posts amplified myths about free speech to discredit opposition to book bans, suppressing protest and deterring participation. This isn't just bad civic discourse—it's a power strategy.

The good news is that we can push back.

1. Teach Constitutional Literacy

Programs like iCivics use interactive case law to teach how rights evolve. Finland's media literacy curriculum pairs well—teaching students how narratives shape belief. Adults need these tools too, especially in communities targeted by misinformation.

2. Use the Constitution as a Floor, Not a Ceiling

The Constitution sets minimum standards. State laws can go further. Medicare's new drug price negotiation powers are a good example—nothing in the Constitution requires them, but they serve the public interest.

3. Clarify the Structure

Codifying rights, like voting access and campaign finance rules, helps prevent judicial backsliding. Canada's finance model offers a useful roadmap: donation caps, public funding, and strict disclosure rules reduce distortion and enhance trust.

4. Reclaim the Narrative

Trusted voices—veterans like Tammy Duckworth, faith leaders like Rev. William Barber, rural labor organizers—can show that constitutional stewardship doesn't mean idolatry. It means ensuring the framework serves everyone, not just those who wrote it.

VI. Conclusion: The Only Way to Honor a Living Constitution Is to Keep It Alive

Even if you trust the Constitution, reform ensures it serves everyone. The text was never meant to be a monument—it was meant to be a mechanism.

Rights aren't granted by paper. They're preserved by people. And when the myths we carry keep us passive, the system stops answering to us. Reform isn't disrespect. It's stewardship.

How the Courts Took Power They Were Never Meant to Hold

Judicial Supremacy, Constitutional Gridlock, and the Roadblock to Reform

In the American civics mythology, the judiciary is supposed to be the "least dangerous branch." It has no army, no budget, and no way to enforce its rulings except by public trust. But in modern America, it has quietly become the most powerful—and the least accountable.

At a time when the public is demanding urgent action on climate, guns, voting rights, and reproductive autonomy, courts are not just interpreting laws. They are blocking them. Worse, the very document they interpret—the U.S. Constitution—is so difficult to amend that even overwhelming public support for reform can be rendered moot. Together, judicial supremacy and constitutional rigidity form a chokepoint where democracy itself goes to die.

This chapter explores how the courts became the final word on nearly everything, why the Constitution resists democratic change, and how other countries—and a few U.S. states—have built more flexible, more accountable systems.

I. The Rise of Judicial Supremacy

When *Marbury v. Madison* established judicial review in 1803, it granted courts the authority to strike down laws that violated the Constitution. But it didn't make the judiciary supreme. For much of U.S. history, courts were a check—not the final say.

That changed slowly over the 20th century, especially after landmark rulings like *Brown v. Board*, which rightly overturned segregation, and *Roe v. Wade*, which expanded privacy rights. But over time, the courts' expanding role in shaping political outcomes turned them into unelected veto points on nearly every contentious issue.

Today, a handful of lifetime-appointed judges can:

- Overturn voter protections (*Shelby County v. Holder*),
- Unleash unlimited campaign spending (*Citizens United*),
- Revoke abortion rights (*Dobbs v. Jackson*),
- Strike down environmental protections (*West Virginia v. EPA*).

And they do so without any real democratic accountability.

II. The Constitution Is Too Rigid to Fix Itself

One reason the courts now dominate public life is that the

Constitution itself can no longer be changed through democratic means. Article V requires a two-thirds vote of Congress and ratification by three-fourths of states. In a hyperpolarized nation, this is politically impossible.

As a result, we no longer amend the Constitution—we litigate it.

This creates a paradox: the only way to adapt the Constitution to modern needs is through the one branch of government that nobody elected and nobody can easily remove. Our democracy depends not on our votes, but on how nine lawyers read a centuries-old document.

Globally, this is unusual:

- **Canada** allows legislatures to override court rulings temporarily through its "notwithstanding clause."

- **Germany** limits judicial terms and subjects constitutional interpretation to a broader framework of evolving democratic norms.

- **New Zealand** adapts through democratic legislation rather than judicial finality.

Even within the United States, states like **Florida** and **South Dakota** allow for citizen-led ballot initiatives that effectively override legislative or judicial inaction. There are democratic tools available—we just don't use them at the federal level.

III. The Court Is Not a Referee. It's a Player-Coach.

Lifetime tenure, ideological vetting, and partisan appointments have made the Supreme Court less like a referee and more like an unelected super-legislature. And because amending the Constitution is a dead end, every major political faction now sees the judiciary as the real seat of power.

This creates perverse incentives:

- Nomination battles become ideological proxy wars.

- Legislators avoid tough votes, expecting courts to "settle" divisive issues.

- Judges strike down policies supported by majorities—often on procedural grounds masked as constitutional interpretation.

And litigation itself is not class-neutral. Access to elite legal teams, coordinated amicus briefs, and long-term strategy is available only to the wealthiest actors. Courts do not just hear cases—they hear the cases that the elite can afford to bring.

IV. What About the Defenses of Judicial Power?
"Courts protect minority rights."

Sometimes. *Obergefell v. Hodges* advanced LGBTQ+ rights. But courts also upheld slavery, legalized segregation, and gutted the Voting Rights Act. A functioning democracy shouldn't depend on the moral compass of nine unelected judges.

"The Constitution should be hard to change to prevent mob rule."
There's a difference between stability and paralysis. When basic reforms—like expanding voting access or guaranteeing reproductive freedom—are blocked for decades, gridlock becomes its own form of oppression.

"Judicial expertise ensures objectivity."
Legal training provides procedural rigor, not ideological neutrality. Judges bring worldviews to the bench, and their "expertise" often mirrors elite interests—as seen in deregulatory rulings shaped by Federalist Society pipelines.

"Wealthy donors are just using courts to seek justice."
Some may believe that. But fossil fuel lobbies and anti-labor groups fund strategic litigation to entrench their influence, long after voters have rejected their policy agendas.

V. Structural Outcomes: When Reform Becomes Impossible

Because the Constitution is nearly unchangeable, and the courts are now its sole editors, we get a system where:

- Voters elect candidates who promise reform—only to see

courts strike it down.

- Agencies like the EPA or SEC are hamstrung by novel legal theories like the "major questions doctrine."
- Congress, paralyzed by gridlock, becomes a spectator to judicial policymaking.

Consider *West Virginia v. EPA*: fossil fuel interests worked through Koch-aligned groups like the **Federalist Society**, funding amicus briefs and legal talent to weaken the EPA's authority. The goal wasn't clarity. It was sabotage by judicial proxy.

This is not how representative democracy is supposed to function. It's how elite rule preserves itself under the veneer of legalism.

VI. What Other Countries—and Some U.S. States—Do Better

- **Canada's "notwithstanding clause"** gives legislatures temporary override power, preventing courts from permanently blocking majority-backed laws.
- **Germany's 12-year term limits** ensure constitutional judges do not wield indefinite influence and are accountable to evolving democratic norms.
- **New Zealand's legislative primacy** ensures that elected officials—not courts—remain the primary drivers of policy change.

- **U.S. state-level ballot initiatives**, like those in Florida and South Dakota, allow for direct democratic correction of elite gridlock and judicial obstruction.

These are not theoretical models. They are real-world tools other democracies use—and that Americans already use at the state level—to avoid governance by judicial bottleneck.

VII. What Can the U.S. Do About It?

1. **Term limits for Supreme Court justices**
   → *Trade-off*: Critics fear judicial independence erosion, but staggered 18-year terms would preserve continuity while ending lifetime dominance.

2. **Override mechanisms at the federal level**
   → *Trade-off*: Opponents may argue this invites abuse, but carefully scoped override clauses—limited to specific policy areas and requiring supermajority thresholds—can offer democratic flexibility without dismantling checks and balances.

3. **Amendment process reform**
   → Introduce alternative amendment pathways, such as national referenda or state-based supermajority compacts, to bypass congressional paralysis.

4. **Transparency and ethics standards**
   → Codify judicial ethics, require recusal disclosures, and

regulate the "shadow docket" to make the Court more accountable to the public.

5. **Expose and counter elite legal networks**
→ The Koch-funded **Freedom Partners** and allied groups have shaped entire legal doctrines through media campaigns and think tank litigation strategies. Public education and disclosure laws can bring these efforts into the light.

6. **Reframe constitutional interpretation as democratic**
→ Promote a civic vision of the Constitution that evolves through public consent, not just elite precedent. Law should serve the governed, not trap them.

VIII. Conclusion: Courts Were Never Meant to Be Kings

Judicial supremacy and constitutional rigidity are not harmless quirks. They are the structural failure points of American governance—chokepoints where popular will is funneled into silence.

The Constitution should be a foundation, not a fortress. Courts should be guardrails, not steering wheels.

When nine unelected justices can override majoritarian reform—and when a centuries-old document can't be changed without elite permission—what we have is not a democracy. It's a stage play of one.

Other countries adapt. Some U.S. states do too.

We can as well.

Support groups like **Demand Justice** or push for judicial term limits in your state legislature. If democracy is to survive, it must rediscover what self-rule actually means.

How the Two Parties Took Control—and How They Stay There

How the Game is Rigged Before the Ballot

For most of American history, political parties rose and fell. The Federalists disappeared. The Whigs imploded. Populists and Progressives surged and fractured. Third parties came and went. But sometime in the 20th century, the landscape hardened. The United States became a two-party state in practice, if not in law—and it's stayed that way ever since.

The Democrats and Republicans didn't just survive. They entrenched. Today, they hold a monopoly on American political power. They write the rules, control the ballots, dominate the media narrative, and funnel billions through the same donor class. And despite their superficial differences, they share a key interest: keeping any real competition out.

To understand how they pulled that off, we need to look at two things: who these parties are today—and what systems keep them in power.

I. The Democrats: A Coalition of the Educated and the Uneasy

The Democratic Party wasn't always the party of social progress. It began in the early 1800s as the political home of agrarian populism under Andrew Jackson. It backed slavery, fought Reconstruction, and long resisted civil rights. That began to shift with the New Deal in the 1930s, which married working-class economic policy to federal power. In the 1960s, the party pivoted again, embracing civil rights and losing the South to the GOP. By the 1990s, under Bill Clinton, it had largely embraced market liberalism and corporate partnerships.

Today's Democratic Party presents itself as the defender of democracy, diversity, and progress. Its base is broad but fragmented: urban professionals, college-educated voters, Black and Hispanic communities (though that support is slipping), and younger voters under 35. Women—especially unmarried women—form a crucial bloc.

Economically, the party walks a fine line. It talks a populist game on wages, healthcare, and student debt but remains deeply intertwined with tech giants, finance capital, and elite institutions. Major donors include Google, Microsoft, and Meta as well as public-sector unions and universities. The result is a technocratic liberalism that champions social justice language while avoiding direct confrontation with corporate power.

Internally, Democrats are divided. The party's left wing—

led by figures like Bernie Sanders and Alexandria Ocasio-Cortez—pushes for structural change. The establishment, backed by legacy media and institutional donors, prefers incrementalism and stability. That tension defines much of the party's current identity.

II. The Republicans: Populist Rhetoric, Elite Control

The Republican Party was born in the 1850s to oppose the expansion of slavery. After the Civil War, it became the party of Northern business and Reconstruction. By the early 20th century, it had aligned with big business, and under Ronald Reagan, it fused social conservatism with economic deregulation. But the real transformation came in the 2000s and 2010s, when the party base radicalized.

Today's GOP is a coalition of contradictions. Its rhetoric is anti-elite, but its policies remain staunchly pro-corporate. It draws support from rural voters, evangelical Christians, non-college-educated whites, and an increasing number of small-business owners and conservative-leaning Hispanic men. It brands itself as the voice of "real America," while being bankrolled by fossil fuel giants, agribusiness, and billionaire-backed super PACs like Club for Growth.

The Trump era hardened this realignment. Nationalism, border security, and culture war issues now dominate the message. Behind the scenes, however, the GOP remains a reliable tool of the donor class—attacking labor, deregulating industry, and stacking the judiciary. Its current threat lies not in its conservatism, but in its willingness to tilt authoritarian when power is threatened.

III. The Real Problem: The System Isn't Broken. It's Working Exactly as Designed.

Both parties benefit from a set of structural systems that keep them in power. These aren't flaws. They're features. They're the quiet machinery that prevents third parties from rising and shuts down meaningful internal dissent.

1. First-Past-the-Post: How the Rules Eliminate Competition

The U.S. uses a first-past-the-post (FPTP) voting system. That means whoever gets the most votes wins, even if it's not a majority. This setup discourages third-party votes and encourages strategic voting—often against your least preferred candidate, not for your true choice.

Political scientists have long understood the consequences of this structure. Duverger's Law states that FPTP tends to create two dominant parties. But it's not automatic. Countries like Canada and the UK also use FPTP and still support viable third parties. What makes the U.S. uniquely resistant is how this voting system interacts with cultural loyalty, winner-take-all presidential elections, and a long history of legal and institutional gatekeeping.

2. Ballot Access and Debate Rules: Legal Gatekeeping

Getting on the ballot as a third-party candidate isn't just hard. It's designed to be. Signature thresholds, state-by-state rules, and legal fees make it prohibitively expensive. Meanwhile, presidential debates are controlled by the Commission on Presidential Debates, a private body created by the Democratic and Republican parties in 1987. The League of Women Voters, which had previously hosted debates, withdrew in protest, citing excessive party control over debate terms.

The CPD now requires candidates to poll at 15% in five national surveys to qualify—a threshold almost impossible to reach without the very exposure that the debates provide. When Ross Perot was included in the debates in 1992, he won nearly 19% of the vote. In 1996, excluded and facing other challenges like reduced funding and political fatigue, his support dropped to 8.4%. Debate exclusion wasn't the only cause, but it was a major one. Visibility is viability, and the rules are designed to ensure that only the existing powers are visible.

3. Primaries: Democracy in Name Only

Both parties claim to let voters choose their nominees. But primaries are tightly controlled affairs. The Democratic Party still includes superdelegates—unpledged party officials and insiders who can vote at the national convention. In 2018, the DNC limited their power by preventing them from voting on the first ballot unless a candidate already has a majority. That reform reduced their ability to override voters directly, but their very presence still signals insider control.

Meanwhile, party rules, delegate allocation games, and early media narratives shape outcomes long before a single vote is cast. "Electability" becomes a self-fulfilling prophecy. Candidates without institutional backing rarely survive the first few contests.

4. Gerrymandering: Safe Seats, No Accountability

Legislative districts are redrawn every ten years. In most states, the party in power draws the map. That means politicians choose their voters, not the other way around.

The result is a vast number of "safe seats" where the only real contest is the primary. That rewards extremism and discourages compromise. Republicans have wielded this tool aggressively since gaining control of many state legislatures in 2010, especially in states like Wisconsin, North Carolina, and Texas. But Democrats have done the same in places like Illinois and Maryland.

The Supreme Court's 2019 ruling in *Rucho v. Common Cause* declared that partisan gerrymandering was beyond its jurisdiction—essentially leaving it up to states. However, the Court still reviews cases involving racial gerrymandering, which remains legally distinct.

5. Dark Money and the Donor Class

Thanks to the Supreme Court's Citizens United decision, unlimited political spending by outside groups is legal. That means billionaires and corporations can fund campaigns through super PACs and dark money networks with no transparency.

Lobbyists write legislation. Industry insiders run regulatory agencies. Lawmakers leave Congress and walk into seven-figure lobbying jobs. This revolving door keeps the system closed. And it ensures that both parties, regardless of rhetoric, serve many of the same interests.

6. Media Concentration and Algorithmic Control

The average American consumes over seven hours of media per day. You might think that creates space for diverse perspectives—but nearly everything you see is owned, filtered, or framed by a handful of corporations. As of the early 2020s, just six companies controlled about 90% of U.S. legacy media: Comcast, Disney, Warner Bros. Discovery, Paramount Global, Fox Corporation, and Sony, though digital platforms have since reduced their dominance.

These conglomerates own hundreds of subsidiary networks —from CNN and MSNBC to Fox News and ABC affiliates. Even alternative-seeming platforms like Hulu or ESPN fall under the same umbrellas. Since then, digital platforms like YouTube, TikTok, and Substack have further fragmented the media landscape. But control hasn't vanished—it's shifted. Algorithms now act as curators, prioritizing outrage, confirmation bias, and engagement loops over complexity or dissent.

Local journalism, once a check on national groupthink, has been gutted. More than 2,500 local papers have closed since 2005.

7. Cultural Habits and Party Identity

The system isn't only held in place by laws and gatekeepers. It's reinforced by culture. Americans are conditioned to think politically in binary terms—red vs. blue, left vs. right. Over time, those affiliations have hardened into personal identity. To vote outside your party isn't just a political risk. It feels like a betrayal.

Cable news and social media deepen that divide. Algorithms favor tribal content and outrage, pushing voters further into partisan silos. The result isn't just preference—it's partisanship as identity, where alternatives aren't considered because they aren't even seen as valid.

IV. Ranked Choice Voting: A Structural Escape Hatch

There is one electoral reform that could break the two-party chokehold without requiring a constitutional amendment or violent upheaval: **ranked choice voting** (RCV). It's not a magic bullet—but it changes the incentives that keep the current system frozen.

In ranked choice systems, voters rank candidates in order of preference. If no one gets a majority, the lowest-performing candidate is eliminated, and those votes are redistributed based on second choices. This repeats until someone crosses 50%.

The key advantage: voters are no longer punished for supporting a third party. That single shift removes the penalty for exploring alternatives and makes room for new parties outside the usual ideological rivalry.

RCV has already been adopted in Maine and in cities like New York and San Francisco. Early evidence shows it reduces negative campaigning and increases voter satisfaction. But it hasn't yet produced third-party breakthroughs in major races. RCV is promising—but it must be paired with campaign finance reform, ballot access relief, and deeper cultural change to make a lasting difference.

V. Conclusion: The Cage Is Real, and It's Locked from the Inside

This isn't a system designed to respond to public will. It's a system designed to absorb it, redirect it, and neutralize it. Both major parties benefit from the status quo. They compete for control of the steering wheel—but neither will let anyone else touch the keys.

Real change won't come from within. It will require external pressure: new laws, new voting systems, and a public willing to see beyond the false choice of Democrat vs. Republican. Until then, we aren't choosing between two visions of the future. We're choosing which gatekeeper gets to keep the door shut.

How the Wealthy Cut Their Taxes and Made Sure It Stayed That Way

The Long Con of Trickle Down Economics

When Americans talk about the rich not paying taxes, they are not hallucinating. They are describing the history of the last fifty years.

In the 1950s and early 1960s, the top federal income tax rate was 91 percent. Corporate taxes sat around 50 percent. Even capital gains — profits from investments like stocks and real estate — were taxed at 25 percent. It was expensive to be rich, at least if you were playing by the rules. That was not an accident. After the Great Depression, American policy makers designed the system to discourage excessive accumulation at the top.

Things began to shift in the early 1970s. Nixon ended the last ties between the dollar and gold in 1971, unleashing a decade of inflation. Prices went up, salaries went up, and because tax brackets were not adjusted for inflation yet, millions of middle-class Americans got pushed into higher tax brackets. This "bracket creep" made federal taxes unpopular across a broad swath of voters. Inflation also hurt people holding fixed assets, creating pressure among the wealthy to find a way out.

In 1978, Congress cut the capital gains tax rate from 39 percent to 28 percent. The argument was that lower capital gains taxes would stimulate investment and economic growth. In practice, it kicked off a new era where owning assets became much more profitable than earning a paycheck.

Then came Reagan. His 1981 tax cuts slashed the top marginal income tax rate from 70 percent to 50 percent. Five years later, the Tax Reform Act of 1986 dropped it again to 28 percent. At the same time, Reagan eliminated many deductions and loopholes that had previously softened the blow for middle-class earners. This was marketed as tax "simplification." It was, but it simplified the system in a way that heavily benefited people at the top.

A few rollbacks happened. Bush Sr. nudged the top income tax rate up to 31 percent in 1990. Clinton raised it to 39.6 percent in 1993. However, capital gains taxes stayed low, preserving the advantage for wealth tied up in assets rather than wages.

In the early 2000s, Bush Jr. pushed another round of tax cuts. The top income tax rate fell to 35 percent. The capital gains tax dropped to 15 percent. If you were rich enough to live off investments, you barely paid anything compared to your personal income tax liability.

Obama reversed some of these cuts after 2012. He added a 3.8 percent Net Investment Income Tax on passive investment income for high earners and restored the top income tax rate to 39.6 percent. It helped a little, but it did not change the overall structure.

Trump's 2017 tax law lowered the top income tax rate again, this time to 37 percent. It slashed corporate taxes permanently from 35 percent to 21 percent. It left the capital gains structure alone, meaning the asset-owning wealthy remained in the best tax position of any class in the country.

Today, after deductions, shelters, and legal tax avoidance strategies, many billionaires pay between 8 percent and 23 percent effective federal tax rates. This is lower than what many middle-class workers pay, and it was built deliberately over decades.

The Capital Gains Loophole

The "capital gains loophole" is a shorthand term for the structural advantage that investment income has over wage income in the United States. Capital gains — profits made from selling assets like stocks, real estate, and businesses — are taxed at lower rates than wages or salaries.

Long-term capital gains, which apply to assets held for over a year, are taxed at a maximum of 20 percent federally. For the wealthiest investors, an additional 3.8 percent Net Investment Income Tax applies. That is still far lower than the top rate on earned income.

But it gets better for the rich. If an investor never sells an asset, they never realize a taxable gain. This is called "unrealized capital gains." Wealthy individuals can borrow against these assets, using them as collateral. They get cash without triggering a taxable event. This "Buy, Borrow, Die" strategy means someone can accumulate enormous wealth, live off loans, and pass the assets to heirs. When the original owner dies, under current law, the assets get a "step-up in basis" — meaning any gains during their lifetime are wiped clean for tax purposes. The heirs inherit the assets as if they were purchased at current market value, tax-free.

In short, the capital gains system does not just lower taxes. It often eliminates them entirely for those rich enough to play the game.

Wealth Preservation Strategies

The capital gains preference is just the start. There are entire industries dedicated to making sure the wealthy keep what they have. Here are some of the most important strategies.

1. Trusts and Foundations

Wealthy individuals often use trusts to transfer assets while avoiding estate taxes. A properly structured trust can shield assets from both taxes and creditors. Foundations allow individuals to shift large amounts of money into vehicles that preserve control while offering charitable tax deductions.

2. Real Estate Depreciation

Real estate investors can deduct "depreciation" on their properties, even as the properties often rise in market value. This paper loss can offset real income, drastically lowering tax bills. When the property is sold, sophisticated investors use "1031 exchanges" to roll the proceeds into new investments, deferring capital gains taxes indefinitely.

3. Offshore Accounts and Shell Companies

Despite crackdowns, offshore accounts and international shell companies still allow the wealthy to shelter money outside U.S. jurisdiction. Moving money through complicated layers of ownership obscures who owns what and where it is taxable.

4. Carried Interest Loophole

Private equity and hedge fund managers often get paid through "carried interest," which is taxed as capital gains rather than ordinary income. This allows them to pay half the tax rate on their earnings compared to a doctor or engineer.

5. Life Insurance Wrappers

Some ultra-wealthy individuals use life insurance policies that bundle investments inside them. The growth inside the policy is tax-deferred, and withdrawals can be structured to avoid taxes entirely. Death benefits pass to heirs tax-free.

Why It Matters

The idea behind preferential treatment for capital gains was to encourage investment and economic growth. In practice, it has supercharged wealth concentration. Asset holders — already disproportionately wealthy — have seen their after-tax returns skyrocket, while wage earners pay closer to full freight.

Efforts to fix the system often crash into political reality. Raising top income tax rates alone will not solve the problem if capital gains and wealth transfers are left intact. True reform would require taxing unrealized gains, ending step-up in basis, closing carried interest loopholes, and curbing the abuse of trusts and foundations.

Without that, the gap will keep growing. It will not happen because of some hidden hand. It will happen because it was engineered to work that way. Once you see it, you cannot unsee it.

Rigged from the Start: Why Our Elections Don't Represent Us—And How to Fix Them

The Hidden Mechanics Behind Voter Powerlessness

American elections are often framed as a celebration of democracy. Citizens go to the polls, votes are counted, and the people choose their leaders. But this story masks a quieter truth: for millions of voters, the outcomes are already decided before they cast a ballot. Not because of fraud or conspiracy—but because of how the districts are drawn and the rules are written.

Gerrymandering and outdated electoral systems have quietly gutted the representative power of the American vote. Instead of competition, we get foregone conclusions. Instead of voter choice, we get party manipulation. Instead of responsive government, we get entrenchment.

Fixing this won't be easy. But if we want a democracy that actually reflects the will of the people, we have to stop pretending our current system was designed to be fair in the first place—and start replacing it with one that is.

I. Gerrymandering: Legal Voter Suppression in Plain Sight

Gerrymandering is the practice of drawing voting district lines to benefit one party over another. It's not new, and it's not subtle. Both Republicans and Democrats have used it to protect incumbents and marginalize opposition. But in recent decades, the precision has grown exponentially thanks to computer modeling and granular voter data.

Consider North Carolina. In 2018, Republican candidates for the U.S. House won just over 50% of the statewide vote—but secured 10 of 13 congressional seats. How? District lines that packed and cracked Democratic voters to ensure a GOP advantage.

The result is a map that doesn't reflect public will—it engineers it.

Some defenders argue that partisan redistricting is just the spoils of political competition. Win the legislature, draw the map. But this ignores the deeper consequence: noncompetitive elections. In gerrymandered districts, general elections become formalities. Primaries, dominated by the most ideologically extreme voters, become the only contest that matters. That incentivizes polarization and punishes compromise.

Even politicians in safe districts occasionally reach across the aisle—especially those with future ambitions—but the dominant trend is clear. Most have little electoral reason to build coalitions when their survival depends on pleasing a narrow base.

II. First-Past-the-Post: Winner-Take-All, Loser-Represented-By-Nobody

Even in districts that aren't gerrymandered, America's winner-take-all voting system creates its own distortions.

In most U.S. elections, the candidate with the most votes wins—even if that's only a small plurality. A Democrat wins a seat with 38% of the vote? The 62% who preferred someone else get nothing. No proportional voice. No shared representation. Just silence.

This is a system designed not for fairness, but simplicity. It's why third parties rarely gain traction and why millions of Americans feel politically homeless. Your choices are constrained not by your beliefs, but by who has a mathematical shot at winning under an archaic model.

Some defenders of first-past-the-post argue it produces stable governments, and avoids the messiness of coalition politics. But stability at the expense of representation isn't democratic—it's calcification. And it's not clear that our current Congress, marked by gridlock and dysfunction, is all that "stable" in practice.

III. Real Alternatives, Already Working

Other countries don't do it this way—and they're not

suffering for it.

Proportional representation systems, where parties win seats in proportion to their share of the vote, are standard in much of the democratic world. Germany, New Zealand, and Sweden all use some form of it, and enjoy higher voter turnout and more ideologically diverse legislatures.

Maine has adopted ranked-choice voting statewide, allowing voters to rank candidates in order of preference. If no one wins a majority, the lowest-polling candidate is eliminated and votes are redistributed until someone does. This discourages negative campaigning and lets voters choose their true favorite without fear of "spoiling" the race.

Meanwhile, states like California, Arizona, and Michigan have created independent redistricting commissions—panels of citizens who draw fairer maps with public input. Michigan's commission, passed by voter initiative in 2018, has already made the state's elections more competitive and representative.

None of these systems are perfect. Proportional representation can lead to fragmented legislatures. Independent commissions can be accused of bias. But these challenges are manageable—and far less damaging than the current status quo.

IV. Why It Hasn't Changed

If better systems exist, why haven't we adopted them?

The short answer: power protects itself. Gerrymandering and winner-take-all voting keep incumbents safe, donors happy, and party leadership in control. Political consultants make fortunes optimizing maps and turnout models. Partisan majorities have every incentive to block reforms that would dilute their grip.

These forces are entrenched. But not invincible. Michigan passed its redistricting reform through a ballot initiative, bypassing a hostile legislature. Maine's ranked-choice voting was approved by voters directly. Grassroots campaigns have proven they can beat institutional resistance—especially when the public understands what's at stake.

V. What Reform Looks Like—and What It Takes

Changing the system means building new structures from the ground up. Here's what that could include:

- **Proportional Representation:** Systems like mixed-member or single transferable vote ensure minority voices aren't drowned out. Critics worry about unstable coalitions, but countries like Germany show that with clear rules, coalition governance can be stable, efficient, and more representative than our current model.

- **Ranked-Choice Voting:** Already working in Maine and dozens of U.S. cities, ranked-choice encourages consensus candidates and lowers the temperature of campaigns.

- **Independent Redistricting Commissions:** These commissions are not perfect, but states like Arizona and Michigan show they're better than letting politicians choose their own voters. Transparent selection processes, public hearings, and strict anti-gerrymandering criteria can build trust.

- **Ballot Initiatives:** When legislatures won't act, citizens can —through state-level initiatives. That's how reform has happened in nearly every successful case so far.

Critics will claim these reforms are confusing, unnecessary, or vulnerable to abuse. But the real threat isn't complexity—it's stagnation. Every year we delay reform, the incentives for dysfunction grow stronger.

VI. The Real Stakes—and What You Can Do

The shape of democracy is drawn on a map before a single vote is cast. That map determines not just who wins, but who is heard, who is silenced, and what issues ever make it to the floor.

We don't need to accept this as normal. We can build a system where representation means something. Where votes translate into voices. Where compromise is rewarded, not punished.

To do that, we need action:

- Support groups like FairVote, RepresentUs, and state-level reform campaigns.

- Vote for local and state candidates who support redistricting reform and voting system changes.

- Talk about these issues. Most Americans don't realize how much the system is rigged by design.

Gerrymandering and electoral distortion aren't side issues. They are the system behind the system.

And the lines we draw now will determine who has a voice in the future.

Why Don't Americans Vote? And What We Can Do About It

Systemic Barriers to Participation

In 2020, 66% of eligible American voters cast a ballot (U.S. Census Bureau). Just two years later, that figure dropped to 46% for the 2022 midterms (Pew Research Center). Local elections often see turnout in the teens. By comparison, countries like Belgium and Sweden regularly exceed 80% turnout (OECD), thanks to automatic registration, trust in institutions, and in some cases, mandatory voting.

This isn't a failure of individual character. It's a failure of design. Voting in the United States is a systemic barrier, not a natural outcome of democratic life. And that's by design—because when fewer people vote, those already in power stay in power.

I. What Keeps People from Voting?

Commentators often cite apathy, but the data tells a different story. Many Americans want to vote—and feel guilty or frustrated when they can't. They don't skip elections because they don't care. They skip because life gets in the way.

The reasons are both practical and psychological:

- Long work hours without paid time off.

- Lack of childcare.

- Poor access to polling places, especially in rural or marginalized urban areas.

- Confusing registration deadlines that vary by state.

Economic pressures compound these challenges. Gig workers with unpredictable schedules, parents balancing multiple jobs, and hourly employees who can't afford to miss a shift often face the most obstacles. The higher your income and the more flexibility you have, the easier it is to vote.

Young voters, in particular, face logistical and psychological hurdles—frequent moves, confusing registration systems, and a digital-first worldview that doesn't align with paper ballots and polling stations. Many are disillusioned by a system that seems impervious to their participation.

Cynicism is often earned—voters see elections yield minimal change as corporations dominate policy—but misinformation and limited civic education can amplify this disconnect. If we want turnout, we need to change the system, not just the messaging.

II. Suppression Still Shapes the System

Many of the most potent voter suppression tactics are

subtle—and legal. They include:

- **Strict Voter ID Laws**: Suppress turnout without reducing fraud, which is already vanishingly rare (Loyola Law School, 2014). Some voters perceive ID laws as trust-building, but that concern is better addressed through transparent audits, not barriers

- **Unlike many U.S. states, Australia does not impose strict voter ID requirements.**
  Voters identify themselves with basic details like name, address, and signature—balancing election security with accessibility.
  This inclusive approach reduces disenfranchisement and ensures that marginalized groups—including the elderly, students, and Indigenous populations—can participate without unnecessary barriers.

- **Voter Roll Purges**: Ostensibly about "cleaning up the rolls," these often remove legitimate voters, disproportionately affecting communities of color and low-income neighborhoods.

- **Limited Polling Places**: Especially in dense urban or rural communities, creating long lines and discouraging participation.

- **Felony Disenfranchisement**: As of 2020, over 4.6 million

Americans were barred from voting due to felony convictions (Sentencing Project), though state reforms may have reduced this number by 2025.

- **Gerrymandering**: Dilutes the power of certain communities by redrawing district lines to predetermine outcomes, discouraging participation by making votes feel meaningless.

These aren't just artifacts of the past. They're ongoing tactics that shape every election.

III. Who Benefits from Low Turnout?

Low turnout primarily benefits incumbents, corporations, and lobbyists by skewing the electorate toward older, wealthier voters. Even progressive incumbents and advocacy groups may leverage low-participation primaries in safe districts. The common thread is that those already in power face less accountability when fewer people vote.

Australia requires citizens to vote by law. Those who fail to vote without a valid reason receive a small fine—typically around AU$20. Despite this, voters are not coerced into endorsing any candidate; they can submit a blank or invalid ballot if they choose. This legal structure has resulted in consistently high voter turnout rates exceeding 90%. It offers a stark contrast to the U.S., where turnout often hovers around 60–66% in major elections and is plagued by participation gaps across demographics.

And as turnout falls, the system reinforces itself. Politicians cater to the smaller group that *does* vote—typically whiter, older, and more affluent. That leads to policies that maintain the status quo, discouraging future participation. It's a feedback loop, and breaking it requires more than asking nicely.

IV. What Would Raise Turnout?

We know what works—because we've seen it succeed in states that have tried.

Here are seven reforms that could structurally improve turnout:

1. **Automatic Voter Registration (AVR)**
   Register eligible citizens when they interact with government agencies, like the DMV. States with AVR have seen registration rates rise by 5–12% (Brennan Center). It eliminates red tape and reduces human error.

2. **Same-Day Registration**
   Let voters register and vote at the same time. States like Maine have boosted turnout by 2–5% using this system (Brennan Center).

3. **Make Election Day a National Holiday & Expand Vote-by-Mail**

Combining time off with flexible voting options reduces logistical barriers for working people.

4. **Secure Smartphone Voting Pilots**

   Estonia's national elections already use secure online voting, backed by biometric ID and blockchain audits. U.S. military e-voting pilots and West Virginia's 2018 blockchain-based voting test for overseas voters show this is possible. While cybersecurity risks and distrust—especially after 2020—are real, municipal-level pilots, paired with bipartisan oversight and transparent audits, could validate security and build trust.

5. **Restore Rights for Former Felons**

   Reinstate voting rights for those who've served their time. This would re-enfranchise millions—particularly Black Americans—while correcting a legacy of racial injustice.

6. **Public Accountability for Suppressors**

   Empower independent watchdogs to challenge state laws that suppress turnout. Lawsuits from groups like the ACLU have been instrumental; codifying this power could deter future suppression.

7. **Digital Civic Education Campaigns**

   Counter disinformation with truth. Target youth through platforms like YouTube, X, and TikTok. Pair with campus voting centers and mobile registration apps. Rebuilding trust requires visibility, transparency, and language that meets voters where they are.

V. Addressing Feasibility and Trust

Yes, some reforms are easier to implement than others. AVR, same-day registration, and vote-by-mail have already succeeded in many states. Smartphone voting and national standards will face political resistance, legal complexity, and cybersecurity scrutiny.

But progress doesn't have to be federal at first. Municipal pilots, ballot initiatives, and public pressure campaigns can lay the groundwork. And if trust is the hurdle, transparency must be the bridge. That means open audits, bipartisan testing, and visible accountability—not just for technology, but for the people and policies shaping the system.

VI. Turnout Is the Structural Outcome

Voter turnout isn't a personal failure—it's a reflection of institutional design. A system that complicates access, suppresses participation, and rewards disillusionment gets exactly the turnout it wants.

But that structure isn't permanent. We can revise it.

Rather than guilting nonvoters, we must remove systemic

barriers through reforms like automatic registration and secure digital voting, ensuring that turnout becomes a tool of accountability—not a casualty of exclusion.

Who Exactly IS the Deep State Again?

Bureaucratic Inertia, Administrative Capture, and the "Deep State" Illusion

The phrase "deep state" has become a catchall for institutional distrust. It evokes an exaggerated image: shadowy bureaucrats, untouched by elections, manipulating government from behind the scenes. But while that narrative overshoots the mark, it isn't born of pure fiction. It reflects a real truth: many Americans feel disconnected from how government works—and frustrated by how slowly it responds to public needs.

That feeling doesn't require conspiracy. It's what happens when institutions are built to avoid risk, reward insiders, and delay reform by design.

I. The Myth That Explains the Malaise

The "deep state" idea appeals because it's simple, emotional, and satisfying. It explains government failures as sabotage instead of dysfunction, turning disappointment into righteous fury. It's no surprise that public confidence has fallen after the financial crisis, costly wars, and a pandemic response riddled with contradictions.

But the core problem isn't a secret cabal—it's public systems designed to be slow. Bureaucratic structures that once promised stability now guarantee paralysis. And when those systems are visibly captured by private interests—regulators defer to the industries they oversee, political appointees return to corporate boards—the frustration feels justified.

That anger is often **redirected**, but the root concern isn't wrong: something is broken.

II. Bureaucracy as a Barrier to Reform

Take the Environmental Protection Agency's years-long delay in updating national ozone pollution standards. Despite scientific consensus and broad public support, the revision languished under layers of interagency review, legal risk, and political calculation. The result? Thousands of preventable deaths from respiratory illness—and no one clearly accountable.

Meanwhile, clean energy subsidies—long supported by both economists and voters—have repeatedly stalled in bureaucratic bottlenecks. Years of delay have kept proven emission-cutting measures from being deployed at scale.

The Affordable Care Act's rollout faltered due to agency coordination failures and IT glitches, frustrating public expectations and reinforcing perceptions of incompetence.

Change demands intricate procedural alignment, not merely consensus. And while slow deliberation once ensured stability—as with Social Security's careful rollout—today's inertia often blocks urgent reforms.

III. When Agencies Are Captured, Not Just Clumsy

Delay is one issue. Influence is another.

The Federal Aviation Administration delegated critical safety oversight of the Boeing 737 Max to Boeing itself—a move encouraged by decades of deregulation and cost-cutting. After two fatal crashes, it became clear the agency had effectively been managing itself on paper while letting Boeing write the rules.

This is administrative capture: when regulators serve the industries they're supposed to regulate. It doesn't require bribes or secret meetings. It happens through a revolving door of personnel and priorities. Steven Mnuchin moved from Goldman Sachs to Treasury. Former ExxonMobil lobbyists helped shape federal energy policy. Google public policy advisors now consult on data privacy regulation.

The result isn't a "deep state." It's a shallow one—where wealth and access replace accountability.

IV. Why Reform So Often Fails

Reform attempts often stall—not due to lack of ideas, but

because entrenched processes protect the status quo. A $16 billion VA health record modernization contract was delayed for years by vendor lawsuits and contracting disputes, leaving veterans waiting an average of 115 days for care at the backlog's peak.

Career incentives discourage bold action. Civil servants are penalized for risk-taking, rewarded for caution. Proposals to streamline permitting or modernize technology face agency turf wars and conflicting statutes. And reforms that do pass are often undercut by implementation failures or legal challenges.

Even well-meaning efforts get chewed up by process.

V. Why Populist Shortcuts Backfire

Frustration leads some to call for decisive leadership—someone who can cut through red tape, purge bureaucrats, and push through reform by force. That instinct is understandable. But concentrating power in one office is rarely the solution.

Authoritarian shortcuts may feel efficient, but they usually politicize expertise, weaken oversight, and amplify instability. Agencies purged of experienced staff don't become leaner—they become hollow. The result is less trust, not more.

Even those who want to tear it down deserve a system that proves them wrong—one that's visible, accessible, and accountable.

VI. What Reform Could Look Like

Fixing this doesn't require blowing up the system. It requires remaking how it serves us. Reforms could include:

- **Sunset Clauses with Transparent Review**
  Every major regulation should expire unless reauthorized through public review. Independent evaluators—supported by citizen panels—could assess effectiveness and force legislative reconsideration. Sunset clauses prevent ossification and create structured reform opportunities.

- **Public Dashboards and Digital Engagement Tools**
  Agencies should publish real-time data on rulemaking, backlogs, and budget allocations. Interactive dashboards—like those used in parts of the EU—allow the public to track decisions and submit comments. Risks of abuse can be managed through moderated platforms, third-party oversight, or AI-filtered feedback.

- **Stronger Revolving Door Restrictions**
  Cooling-off periods should be extended for officials moving between regulatory roles and the industries they oversee. Naming specific figures—like Joseph Simons, former FTC chair with prior ties to Big Tech—underscores why clearer boundaries matter.

- **Citizen Oversight Panels**

Randomly selected citizen juries, modeled on Ireland's constitutional process, could audit agencies or review contested rules. Participants would receive expert briefings and be vetted for conflicts of interest, with nonpartisan facilitation to guard against manipulation.

- **Whistleblower Protection and Culture Reform**
  Groups like Whistleblower Aid show how targeted support can elevate insider voices. Legal protections, public recognition, and modest financial safety nets can encourage ethical disclosures and shift internal norms. Think of Frances Haugen at Facebook—not just punished leakers, but civic-minded truth-tellers.

- **Participatory Budgeting for Agencies**
  Pilot programs like Seattle's public budgeting tools show that citizen input can shape spending priorities. Applying this model at the agency level could democratize how public funds are allocated and evaluated.

Some might argue that engaging the public risks populist hijacking or anti-intellectualism. But diverse, randomized selection —paired with expert facilitation—can build legitimacy without inviting chaos.

Others say inertia prevents rash decisions. But today, inertia is protecting failure—not preventing it.

VII. Conclusion: Institutions Should Serve, Not Stifle

The "deep state" is a bad label for a real problem: systems that feel closed, unaccountable, and incapable of meaningful change.

Reform doesn't mean trusting blindly—it means building systems that don't require trust to function. Systems you can see, question, and improve.

Democracy means empowering people to shape the institutions that govern them—not watching from a distance while insiders call the shots.

And the more visible those systems become, the less powerful the myths around them will be.

Tools or Tyrants?

AI, Technology, and the Future of Democratic Reform

In America, technology is near-religion. We assume every new tool brings progress—and every innovation expands freedom. But history tells a more cautionary story. Technology doesn't inherently liberate; it magnifies whatever systems already dominate. AI is no exception. Today, artificial intelligence is reshaping democratic life—not through utopian efficiency, but through biased algorithms, invisible decision-making, and concentrated corporate control. While its advocates promise expanded access and objectivity, the reality is that most AI is optimized for profit, embedded in private infrastructure, and largely shielded from public scrutiny. Rather than leveling the playing field, it risks reproducing—and accelerating—existing forms of inequality.

That doesn't mean the outcome is inevitable. Through transparency, public oversight, and decentralized ownership, AI could become a force for reform. But left to the market, it's more likely to entrench power than disrupt it. Critics of regulation often argue that audits and open data will stifle innovation. But speed without fairness isn't progress. It's privatized control.

I. Technology Isn't Neutral

AI is frequently described as a neutral tool. But tools are only as fair as the systems that wield them. AI reflects human decisions at every step: what data to include, what outcomes to reward, and who gets to challenge the result. When those choices are locked behind proprietary code, accountability vanishes. Control shifts from public institutions to private developers, while affected communities are left without recourse.

This isn't abstract. In 2016, ProPublica found that a widely used risk assessment tool falsely flagged Black defendants as high-risk nearly twice as often as white defendants. A 2020 investigation by AlgorithmWatch revealed that automated hiring platforms replicated gender and racial biases—privileging candidates who resembled existing leadership. And in 2021, the Center for Democracy & Technology documented how content moderation systems disproportionately suppressed political dissent and satire, particularly from marginalized voices.

Technology doesn't invent injustice. It accelerates it—and obscures it beneath a veneer of objectivity.

II. The False Promise of AI as Reform

One of AI's most seductive promises is bureaucratic efficiency. By replacing slow, expensive government processes with streamlined automation, reformers claim, we can eliminate waste and error. But automation often expands bureaucracy instead of shrinking it—and does so without accountability.

Consider Michigan's MIDAS system, launched in 2013 to flag unemployment fraud. It falsely accused over 34,000 people of criminal behavior. Many were denied benefits without warning and left with no meaningful way to appeal. Years later, the state was forced to pay out hundreds of millions in settlements. In Wisconsin, courts used the COMPAS algorithm to assess recidivism risk. A 2018 ACLU review found that it misclassified defendants in ways that deepened racial disparities, all while hiding its internal logic from public scrutiny.

Across the U.S., agencies are quietly testing AI for everything from benefits processing to housing allocation to legislative drafting. Few of these programs include audit trails, public feedback, or transparent criteria. The result is automation without justice—faster decisions, but fewer rights.

III. Building Democratic Technology

AI isn't inherently authoritarian. It could just as easily become a tool for reform, if designed with democratic principles in mind. That means transparency in how systems are built and used. It means mandatory disclosure of training data, independent audits of algorithmic decisions, and appeal processes when errors occur. Without those basic safeguards, trust collapses.

Technology can also be used to promote civic engagement. Real-time dashboards powered by AI could display budget allocations, complaint resolution times, or public feedback summaries—offering citizens a clearer view of what their government is doing. These systems already exist in prototype form and could become powerful tools for breaking through bureaucratic inertia.

Some governments are experimenting with participatory platforms that use AI to scale public input. Taiwan's Polis system, for example, helped synthesize citizen feedback during debates over ride-sharing regulation. The outcome wasn't a binary decision but a balanced policy grounded in collective intelligence.

AI can also support anti-corruption efforts. Machine learning can identify rigged contracts, financial anomalies, or revolving-door relationships between regulators and industry. Brazil's Lava Jato ("Car Wash") scandal—which uncovered billions in government fraud—was assisted by data analysis of this kind.

Even the architecture of our digital systems matters.

Decentralized tools—such as federated platforms like Mastodon, or civic blockchain registries—can reduce monopolistic control and return agency to local communities. Publicly governed digital ID systems could streamline benefits access without creating surveillance dragnets. These technologies already exist. The question isn't whether they work—it's whether we choose to scale them in the public interest, or let corporate platforms define the rules.

IV. What We Risk If We Don't Act

If we fail to reform AI now, we risk hard-coding inequality into the infrastructure of everyday life. Institutions that already lack transparency will become black boxes. Surveillance will be normalized—from face scans at protests to behavioral scores in schools. Deepfakes, filtered content, and algorithmic manipulation will distort public understanding of reality. And elections will be shaped not by open debate, but by hyper-targeted campaigns designed to divide and suppress.

These trends aren't hypothetical. They're already underway. The longer we wait, the harder it becomes to retrofit these systems with democratic guardrails. Power, once centralized, does not give itself up easily.

V. Conclusion: AI is a Force Multiplier

AI doesn't fix broken systems. It amplifies them. If a

process is opaque, AI will make it more so. If it's biased, AI will scale the bias. If it's corrupt, AI will entrench the corruption faster and deeper than any human bureaucracy could manage.

The solution isn't to fear the technology—it's to govern it. That requires building structures that favor citizens over surveillance, participation over manipulation, and fairness over speed. Democracy isn't a relic. It's a design challenge.

And like any design challenge, it's only as good as the tools we choose to build with.

Artificial Influence: How Corporate Personhood Distorted Democracy

What happens when we confuse a corporation for a citizen?

I. Introduction: The Rulebook Wasn't Neutral

In the United States, we often treat our democracy as if it's a level playing field—where ideas compete fairly, elections are honest, and public will guides public policy. But the rulebook wasn't written by the public. Many of its most important provisions were shaped by private interests with deep pockets and long reach.

At the center of this distortion is corporate personhood—a legal fiction that gives corporations many of the rights of individuals. What began as a limited protection has become a structural advantage, one that allows immense concentrations of wealth to manipulate elections, draft legislation, and drown out the will of actual citizens.

This chapter examines how corporate personhood emerged, how campaign finance became its most powerful tool, and why serious structural reform is necessary to restore democratic accountability.

II. The Origins of Corporate Personhood

Corporate personhood was not designed to confer political power. In the 19th century, courts extended limited rights to corporations so they could sue, be sued, and enter contracts. These were economic tools—not democratic privileges.

But in **Santa Clara County v. Southern Pacific Railroad (1886)**, a passing comment by the Court's headnote—never part of the official ruling—suggested that corporations were protected under the 14th Amendment. That phrase, though legally non-binding, became precedent. And over the next century, corporations leveraged it to claim broader constitutional rights—culminating in full First Amendment protections.

What began as a technical convenience was transformed into political leverage. The question wasn't just whether corporations had legal standing. It became whether their money counted as speech—and whether limiting their spending was tantamount to censorship.

III. Citizens United and the Unleashing of Dark Money

The turning point came with **Citizens United v. FEC** in 2010. The ruling held that corporations and unions could spend unlimited sums to influence elections, provided they didn't coordinate directly with campaigns. Political spending, the Court said, was protected speech.

The result was an explosion of Super PACs—technically independent, but often functionally aligned with specific candidates. These groups collect and spend unlimited donations, much of it untraceable through dark-money networks. In 2020 alone, Super PACs spent over $2.1 billion—a level of influence unthinkable before the ruling.

Defenders argue this levels the playing field between corporate and union voices. But this ignores both the scale and direction of influence. Political spending from corporations and their affiliated PACs outpaces union spending by roughly 15 to 1, and union membership continues to decline.

Some also argue that corporations are associations of people, and thus entitled to free speech. But that analogy fails: corporations represent shareholder value, not civic responsibility. They don't vote. They don't serve on juries. They don't face the consequences of the policies they help shape.

IV. Beyond Campaigns: Lobbying, Access, and Narrative Control

Campaign contributions are only one avenue of influence. More quietly, corporate power shapes the content, tone, and priority of the national agenda.

- **Lobbying**: Corporations spend billions annually to shape legislation. The fossil fuel industry, for example, spent over $118 million on lobbying in 2022—much of it to delay or weaken climate action.

- **Pharmaceutical lobbying** helped block Medicare drug price negotiations for years, despite overwhelming public support.

- **Think tanks** funded by corporate donors produce research and talking points that reinforce donor priorities under the veneer of scholarship.

- **Corporate-owned media** amplifies donor-friendly narratives and frames reforms like public health care or labor protections as radical rather than mainstream.

The result is not just tilted elections, but distorted public debate. Many of the most impactful decisions—what policies are considered viable, what bills get written, and what problems are treated as urgent—are shaped long before a vote is cast.

V. Global Comparisons: The U.S. as an Outlier

The United States allows more corporate influence in politics than nearly any other advanced democracy.

- **Canada** bans corporate and union donations to parties.
- **France** limits individual contributions and uses public

financing to level the playing field.

- **Germany** combines proportional representation with strong transparency laws to reduce big-donor control.

These systems are far from perfect. But they offer proof that democratic elections don't require unchecked political spending—or the legal fiction that companies are citizens.

VI. Counterarguments, Addressed

Supporters of corporate personhood argue that spending is speech, and that restricting corporate donations risks silencing legitimate voices. Some claim that corporate spending balances union power, pointing to labor's historical alignment with the Democratic Party.

But these defenses collapse under scrutiny:

- Unions represent workers. Corporations represent capital. Their influence is not equivalent in scale or effect.

- Union membership is shrinking, while corporate revenue and PAC spending continue to grow.

- Campaign finance reform is not censorship—it's a boundary between governance and commerce, between citizens and artificial entities.

- Disclosure doesn't silence speech. It informs voters about who is speaking—and why.

The balance is illusory. The megaphone of corporate money drowns out small donors, distorts elections, and warps policy long before any vote is cast.

VII. Solutions, With Trade-Offs

Fixing this problem requires structural reform. Some options are already underway at the state and local level:

- **Public campaign financing**: Programs like Seattle's **Democracy Vouchers** give each voter public funds to donate to candidates. Concerns about fairness can be addressed through transparent, independent oversight, as Seattle's experience has shown.

- **Overturning Citizens United**: A constitutional amendment is a steep climb, but campaigns like **Move to Amend** have built support in over 20 states.

- **Stronger disclosure laws**: Mandating real-time donor transparency—especially for dark-money groups—would let voters see who's behind the ads.

- **Tax and lobbying reforms**: Ending tax deductions for political expenses and closing revolving-door loopholes would help reduce subtle but pervasive influence.

- **Media regulation**: Restoring ownership caps and requiring source transparency would reduce narrative monopolies and broaden the national conversation.

Each solution carries risks. Public financing must be shielded from political capture. Free speech must be preserved even as influence is regulated. But we've done this before. The **Tillman Act (1907)** banned direct corporate donations. **McCain-Feingold (2002)** aimed to close soft-money loopholes before Citizens United blew them open again.

We have precedent. What we lack is political will.

VIII. Conclusion: We Can Redraw the Lines

Corporate personhood is not a natural right. It's a legal fiction—one that's been stretched far beyond its original purpose. When we allow artificial entities to shape real-world governance without democratic accountability, we invite structural failure.

This isn't an abstract issue. It's about who writes the laws, who gets heard, and who gets served.

We don't need to eliminate corporations from civic life. We need to redefine the boundary between profit and power—and restore a basic principle: one person, one voice.

Support campaigns like Move to Amend. Advocate for public financing in your city. Ask your candidates where they get their money—and what they owe in return.

Because a democracy where voters outrank donors isn't just possible. It's necessary.

Faith and the Flag: The Political Capture of Religion in the U.S.

How Christian nationalism became a political machine—and why it's undermining both democracy and faith.

I. This Isn't About God

Let's start here: This is not a critique of belief. It's a critique of power.

Millions of Americans practice their religion quietly and sincerely. That's not the problem. The problem is when religion becomes a political weapon—when elected officials, media networks, and billionaire donors wrap their agendas in scripture and call it sacred.

Christian nationalism is not about faith. It's about control.

II. America Wasn't Founded as a Christian Nation

The myth is persistent: that the U.S. was built on Christian values and should remain a Christian nation. That idea has never been legally true—and was explicitly rejected by the Founders themselves.

The First Amendment draws a clear boundary: "Congress shall make no law respecting an establishment of religion." Thomas Jefferson called it a "wall of separation." James Madison opposed religious taxes and clerical power. The Treaty of Tripoli, ratified in 1797, stated plainly: "the Government of the United States of America is not, in any sense, founded on the Christian religion."

That said, Christianity has clearly shaped American culture. From the Puritan work ethic to the language of civic rituals, Christian norms were deeply embedded in early American life. But the legal structure was intentionally secular—designed to keep government neutral, not faithless.

III. What Christian Nationalism Actually Is

Christian nationalism isn't just religiosity. It's the belief that the U.S. is divinely favored, that Christianity should shape public law, and that pluralism is a threat. It blends fundamentalist theology with hard-right politics and has been deeply embedded into electoral strategy since the late 1970s.

The rise of the Moral Majority in that era, coupled with the politicization of issues like abortion, transformed large evangelical networks into a Republican voting bloc. Groups like the Family Research Council, Liberty Counsel, and Project Blitz have since worked to mainstream this ideology—drafting legislation, influencing school boards, and shaping judicial appointments.

This isn't fringe. It's now a dominant faction inside one of the two major parties.

IV. Mechanisms of Power: Pulpits and Courtrooms

While not all conservative churches endorse Christian nationalism, many have become hubs for its messaging, leveraging their logistical power to shape voter behavior.

Churches offer built-in turnout operations: weekly gatherings, trusted messengers, and tax-exempt platforms for political persuasion. In practice, many congregations function as ideological training grounds, reinforcing narratives about abortion, LGBTQ+ rights, gender roles, and the supposed moral collapse of the nation.

Meanwhile, the courts have become active participants. The Supreme Court has shifted its interpretation of religious freedom from protection to preference. The *Lemon test*, once used to prevent government entanglement with religion, was effectively buried in *Kennedy v. Bremerton* (2022), which upheld a public school football coach's right to lead prayer at the 50-yard line.

In *Burwell v. Hobby Lobby* (2014), the Court allowed corporations to claim religious exemptions from federal healthcare mandates. These decisions don't just protect religious expression— they elevate it above secular law.

This is what soft theocracy looks like: not a state-run religion, but state-enabled theology.

V. Policy by Piety

The policy impacts are sweeping:

- **Reproductive rights** have been curtailed in dozens of states, often justified by religious arguments rather than public health data.

- **LGBTQ+ protections** have been rolled back under the guise of "religious liberty."

- **Public education** is being recast as a battleground, with demands for school prayer, anti-LGBTQ+ curricula, and history rewritten to glorify a Christian past.

- **Federal funding** flows freely to faith-based organizations, often with limited oversight or nondiscrimination enforcement.

Christian nationalism isn't just influencing policy. It's reshaping the architecture of governance.

VI. Who Benefits—and Who's Left Out

Theocracy—even informal—always requires exclusion.

Muslims, Jews, atheists, progressive Christians, and secular citizens are routinely sidelined. When "religious freedom" becomes shorthand for Christian supremacy, everyone else is cast as suspect.

This dynamic marginalizes young people, immigrants, and communities whose identities don't fit a monolithic vision of Christian Americanness.

Progressive Christians, along with interfaith groups like the Poor People's Campaign and Sojourners, have pushed back—advocating for a faith that prioritizes justice over dominance. Some conservative evangelicals, like Russell Moore, have also criticized Christian nationalism as a betrayal of Christian ethics and public witness.

The problem isn't belief. It's the merger of belief and state power.

VII. Why It Works

Christian nationalism's appeal lies in its emotional resonance. It thrives where economic anxiety, cultural alienation, and distrust in institutions leave people searching for certainty. By framing moral decay as the nation's problem—and divine restoration as the solution—it offers a comforting narrative.

It tells people they haven't failed. The nation has. And only God, through the ballot box, can bring it back.

VIII. Counterarguments—and Why They Fail

"America was founded on Christian values."

→ Christianity influenced early American culture, but the Constitution deliberately created a secular government. The Founders rejected state religion precisely because they saw what it had done to Europe.

"This protects religious liberty."

→ Exemptions for individual conscience sound fair, but when they undermine public access to services or healthcare, they prioritize one group's beliefs over everyone else's rights. That's not liberty. That's preference.

"You just hate religion."

→ No. When faith relies on state power, it risks becoming a tool of politics rather than a personal conviction. Faith should be free—not weaponized.

"This is just democracy—majorities set the rules."

→ Democracy protects minorities, not just majorities. When one group's beliefs override others' rights, it's not representation—it's domination.

IX. What Reform Would Actually Look Like

- **Reinforce the Establishment Clause**

    → No public funding for schools or institutions that discriminate under the banner of religion.

- **Audit 501(c)(3) abuse**
  → The IRS could enforce existing rules against partisan politicking, with penalties for churches that function as campaign hubs.

- **Mandate religious transparency**
  → Require disclosure when religious organizations fund litigation, lobbying, or electioneering.

- **Expand civic pluralism education**
  → Programs like the National Constitution Center's civics curriculum could be expanded to include real-world examples of how pluralism and faith coexist.

- **Invest in cultural strategies**
  → Media literacy campaigns, like those piloted by the News Literacy Project, can teach communities to spot politicized religious narratives. Interfaith organizing, such as the Poor People's Campaign's coalition-building, can amplify pluralistic voices and reframe faith as a force for inclusion—not exclusion.

X. Conclusion: Faith Doesn't Need a Flag

For millions, faith is a source of hope and community. Protecting that sincerity means keeping it free from political capture.

Religious liberty depends on boundaries, not dominance. When politicians blur the line between belief and law, they don't elevate faith—they weaponize it. No religion is safe once the state claims to speak for God.

You can love your country and still refuse to baptize your ballot.

For Christians who cherish Jesus's teachings on justice and love, rejecting the political capture of faith is not just a civic duty—it's a moral one.

And whether you're religious or secular, the fight for a pluralistic democracy starts with recognizing this threat—and refusing to let it speak in your name.

You can believe in God and still believe in the First Amendment.

Rewriting the Rules: Legal Reforms That Could Shift American Power

Laws built the current imbalance—and laws can undo it. Here are the ones that matter most.

In American politics, we spend most of our time arguing about *who* should be in power. But we rarely stop to ask *how* power works in the first place.

The real game isn't fought on debate stages or in cable news segments. It's structured—quietly, invisibly—through the laws and rules that decide who gets to participate, how elections are financed, and what information the public receives. These aren't cultural battles. They're legal ones. And the history of reform in this country proves that laws are not sacred. We've changed the rules before—sometimes radically—and we can do it again.

This chapter lays out which laws should be repealed or replaced to restore balance in American democracy, along with real-world reforms that could shift influence away from moneyed gatekeepers and toward the people who are supposed to be represented. None of these proposals are hypothetical. And none of them require fantasy candidates or perfect conditions. Just political will—and clarity.

I. What the Law *Has* Changed Before

America isn't new to legal reform. At multiple points in our history, structural laws have shifted the political playing field—not just for a single party or cycle, but for entire generations.

- **The Voting Rights Act (1965)** dramatically expanded who could vote by establishing federal oversight in states with a history of suppression. For decades, it helped guarantee ballot access—until the Supreme Court weakened it in 2013.

- **The Seventeenth Amendment (1913)** ended the system where U.S. Senators were chosen by state legislatures and handed that power directly to voters. It was a radical shift in democratic access—met with stiff resistance at the time.

- **The Pendleton Act (1883)** created the modern civil service, dismantling the spoils system and turning government jobs into merit-based roles. It professionalized governance and broke one of the most entrenched patronage systems in American history.

- **The GI Bill (1944)**, though flawed in implementation, redistributed power by offering education, home loans, and vocational training to veterans—creating a middle class virtually overnight. Its uneven racial application (Black veterans were often denied benefits due to local discrimination) is a reminder that reform is only as just as its enforcement.

We don't need a fantasy. We need memory. We've done this before.

II. What Should Be Repealed or Reformed

Citizens United v. FEC (2010)

This ruling unleashed a flood of corporate and union spending in elections. Enabled by loopholes in tax law and nonprofit status, it led to the rise of super PACs and "dark money" groups that spend millions without meaningful disclosure.

Some argue that money was always part of politics—and that's true. But Citizens United took a bad situation and broke the floodgates. Between 2012 and 2020, super PAC spending more than doubled, from $1.3 billion to $2.8 billion (OpenSecrets).

Repealing Citizens United wouldn't eliminate money's influence, but it would curb corporate domination and amplify small donors' voices. Changing it would require a new Supreme

Court ruling or constitutional amendment—but public support for campaign finance reform remains high, and state-level models like Maine's Clean Elections system prove alternatives exist.

The Filibuster

The filibuster isn't a law. It's a procedural tactic—but one that's been weaponized to block even basic legislation supported by the majority of Americans.

Historically, it was rarely used. Today, it's standard practice—used to stall voting rights, climate action, gun safety, and nearly every form of structural reform. Supporters say it protects minority rights. In practice, it protects minority rule.

While the filibuster once encouraged compromise, its modern use shields entrenched interests. Reforms like lowering the threshold to 55 votes or requiring a talking filibuster could restore some balance without eliminating it entirely.

The Telecommunications Act (1996)

Sold as modernization, this law allowed massive media consolidation. By 2022, five corporations controlled over 80% of U.S. broadcast and cable TV revenue (Nielsen). Add in Google, Meta, and Amazon, and you have a handful of companies steering the digital conversation—algorithmically amplifying outrage, disinformation, and commercial narratives.

Revising this act and updating Section 230 of the **Communications Decency Act** could help regulate platform algorithms, reduce digital manipulation, and restore local and independent media ecosystems.

III. What Should Be Enacted

Automatic Voter Registration (AVR)

Instead of opting in, voters would be registered automatically when they interact with government systems (e.g., DMV, tax forms), with the ability to opt out.

States that have implemented AVR—like Oregon and Colorado—have seen 5–10% increases in turnout (Brennan Center). AVR would particularly benefit Black, Latino, and younger voters who face disproportionate registration barriers.

Independent Redistricting Commissions

Congressional districts are often drawn by the party in power—a process that allows politicians to choose their voters instead of the other way around.

States like California and Michigan have adopted citizen-led commissions to draw fairer maps. Expanding this nationwide would reduce gerrymandering, restore competitive races, and create districts that better reflect actual communities.

Public Campaign Financing

Under systems like Seattle's "Democracy Vouchers," residents receive small public funds to donate to candidates of their choice. This flips campaign funding from a contest of billionaires to a contest of ideas.

Public financing reduces the power of major donors, elevates working-class candidates, and increases the diversity of political representation—especially for women and people of color. Paired with stricter limits on outside money, it could reset campaign incentives entirely.

Real-Time Financial Transparency

The STOCK Act was supposed to stop insider trading by members of Congress. Instead, it's been ignored with minimal consequences.

Reform should include real-time public disclosures (within 48 hours), mandatory blind trusts, and bans on individual stock ownership for lawmakers. Some critics argue this could discourage middle-class candidates—but reforms can be structured to preserve retirement options while banning active trading during office.

Secure Digital Voting Access

In 2025, most Americans bank, work, and manage healthcare from their smartphones. Voting? Still reliant on limited hours and in-person lines.

Secure digital voting—beginning with small-scale pilots—could expand access, especially for rural, disabled, or working voters. Critics rightly raise cybersecurity concerns. But Estonia has used national e-voting since 2005, and U.S. military e-ballot systems show that secure infrastructure is possible. Transparency, biometric checks, and encrypted audit trails would be key.

Some worry that increased turnout could destabilize predictable voting blocs. But unpredictability is not a flaw—it's a feature of actual democracy.

Judicial Term Limits
The Supreme Court has lifetime appointments, meaning justices can serve for 30–40 years regardless of shifts in public sentiment.

Proposals for 18-year term limits would reduce entrenchment and partisan gaming of retirement timing. Implementation may require legislation or reinterpretation, but could preserve judicial independence while restoring public trust.

IV. Structural Reform Means Nothing Without Enforcement
Every reform here is achievable. But passing a law is only half the battle. Enforcing it is where the system usually breaks down.

- The **Voting Rights Act** lost power because the formula for oversight was invalidated—not because the law disappeared.

- The **STOCK Act** exists, but with no teeth.

- Redistricting commissions can be hijacked without proper oversight.

That's why reforms must be paired with enforceable standards: independent ethics boards, audit trails, financial penalties, and public reporting. Judicial reform must also be part of the conversation, or any new law risks being dismantled from the bench.

Some reforms may also face states' rights pushback. But the Constitution gives Congress the power to regulate elections, and the courts have upheld that authority when paired with civil rights enforcement. State-level wins—like Michigan's redistricting overhaul—prove that local reform can ripple upward.

Economic power matters too. Public financing and antitrust enforcement can work in tandem to ensure that political reforms aren't swallowed by wealth consolidation. Laws that reduce monopolistic media control or limit the political sway of massive donor networks serve the same goal: a government that answers to the public, not to platforms or patrons.

V. The System Is Still a System

Reforms won't create utopia. They won't fix everything. But they change the playing field. They decide who gets heard, who gets funded, and who gets elected. And they outlast politicians.

Forget waiting for saviors. **Rewrite the rules, and we rewrite the future.**

Narrative Control: How Media Consolidation, Social Platforms, and Think Tanks Shrink the Boundaries of American Politics

When five companies, a few billionaires, and a few lines of code decide what's possible, your democracy is already on life support.

I. Introduction: A Narrow Window

In American politics, the most dangerous ideas are not the ones we argue about. They're the ones we never hear.

Public debate is framed as a freewheeling clash of opinions, but the truth is, most of what gets said—by candidates, commentators, or even voters—falls within an invisible perimeter: the Overton window. This is the narrow range of ideas that are considered "acceptable" to discuss in public.

What lies outside that window is not debated—it's ignored, ridiculed, or suppressed.

The boundaries of the window are not defined by logic or evidence. They are enforced by the information ecosystem:

- A media industry dominated by five conglomerates
- Social media platforms whose algorithms reward outrage and tribalism
- A network of elite-funded think tanks that generate justifications for the status quo

This chapter examines how these forces shape, shrink, and control what Americans believe is politically possible—often without them realizing it.

II. Legacy Media: Five Corporations, One Voice

By 2022, five companies controlled over 80% of U.S. broadcast and cable TV revenue (Nielsen), while the remaining outlets fought for scraps. That concentration of power doesn't just reduce the diversity of content—it narrows the range of ideas that make it to the public at all.

Corporate media is not a monolith of ideology; it's a consensus machine. Issues that threaten corporate interests—like antitrust enforcement, wealth redistribution, or public ownership—rarely receive sustained attention. Meanwhile, debates about "wokeness," wardrobe choices, or Biden's stair coordination dominate headlines.

Depth loses to drama.

This isn't accidental. Investigative journalism is expensive. Spectacle is cheap. And when the same parent company owns both the cable news network and a major defense contractor—or an advertising division and a sports network—it's not hard to guess what kind of coverage wins.

Counterpoint: Some argue that media consolidation improves efficiency and quality control. But that logic assumes that "efficiency" in journalism is a virtue. It's not. The goal isn't to streamline information—it's to inform the public and hold power accountable. When five companies decide what qualifies as news, accountability is the first casualty.

III. Social Platforms: The Algorithm as Censor

If legacy media shrinks the Overton window through omission, social media narrows it through distortion. Platforms like X (formerly Twitter), Facebook, and TikTok don't operate by journalistic standards. Their algorithms don't reward accuracy—they reward engagement.

And what drives engagement? Outrage, tribalism, fear.

When a user posts a reasoned, evidence-based thread about healthcare reform, it gets 12 likes. When someone posts a conspiracy theory accusing public officials of satanic crimes, it goes viral. The system isn't malfunctioning. It's working exactly as designed.

Example: In 2020, Facebook's internal research found that algorithmic changes designed to boost "meaningful interaction" had instead amplified inflammatory political content. Content from extremist pages was recommended more frequently than from mainstream news outlets.

Case in point: During the early Black Lives Matter protests, hashtags promoting peaceful organization were repeatedly throttled or de-emphasized, while inflammatory content about looting and violence surged in visibility. Platforms later claimed it was accidental. The pattern said otherwise.

This isn't just noise—it's narrative warfare. When algorithms flood your feed with sensational garbage, they crowd out serious alternatives.

Overton Impact: Algorithms don't just reflect public interest; they shape it. By pushing the most divisive content to the top, they redefine what seems "normal" and what feels "extreme."

IV. Think Tanks: Intellectual Legitimacy for the Status Quo

Not all narrative control is noisy. Some of it wears a suit and writes white papers.

The American policy landscape is crowded with think tanks—Heritage, AEI, Cato, and dozens more—whose role is to produce the appearance of intellectual rigor while promoting donor-friendly policy.

These institutions craft language, fund studies, and supply talking points that shape how media and politicians frame issues. Phrases like "job creators," "school choice," or "fiscal responsibility" are not neutral terms—they are branded concepts developed to shift public opinion and policymaker behavior.

Example: The American Enterprise Institute played a critical role in promoting the Bush-era tax cuts, citing growth projections that later proved wildly optimistic. The Koch-funded Mercatus Center shaped deregulatory policy under multiple administrations, including opposition to net neutrality framed as "pro-innovation."

Why this matters: Think tanks are often staffed by credentialed academics and former government officials. They appear nonpartisan. In reality, many serve as ideological laundering operations—polished, peer-reviewed pathways for elite interests to appear neutral or even populist.

Counterpoint: Some argue that think tanks offer valuable expertise and long-term policy vision that electoral politics often lacks. That's true—when they're genuinely independent. But when institutions rely on billionaire funding and corporate sponsors, their "research" often aligns suspiciously with donor priorities.

Overton Impact: Think tanks don't just reinforce the window—they shift it. By redefining what counts as "serious" or "fiscally responsible," they make meaningful redistribution or structural reform seem radical—even when those ideas are supported by most Americans.

V. Proposed Solutions — and Their Trade-Offs

The structure isn't broken because someone made a mistake. It's broken because it serves powerful interests exactly as intended. Fixing it means changing the incentives—structurally, not sentimentally.

1. Antitrust Enforcement for Media and Platforms

Break up media conglomerates. Challenge mergers between news outlets and unrelated industries. Treat dominant platforms like utilities.

Trade-off: Critics argue this could reduce operational efficiency or spark regulatory overreach. But media is not toothpaste—efficiency must not outweigh public interest.

2. Algorithmic Transparency Laws

Require platforms to disclose how content is ranked, and offer opt-outs from engagement-based feeds.

Trade-off: Platforms may claim proprietary harm, but transparency is essential in any system shaping political opinion at scale.

3. Public Funding for Journalism

Establish independent, publicly funded media with strict insulation from political interference.

Trade-off: Critics fear bias or state propaganda. That's fair—but many democracies (e.g., the UK, Germany, Canada) fund media with safeguards. The U.S. can too.

4. Restoring a Modern Fairness Doctrine

Revive a version of the Fairness Doctrine for broadcast and digital platforms, requiring outlets to label commentary and present competing views.

Trade-off: First Amendment concerns are real. But clearly distinguishing opinion from news is a quality standard, not censorship.

5. Media Literacy Education

Integrate critical media analysis into high school curricula. Teach students how narratives are shaped and by whom.

Trade-off: Implementation takes time. But long-term, nothing changes if people can't tell truth from noise.

6. Disrupt the Funding Stream

Ban political donations from think tanks, require full disclosure of funders, and limit their tax-exempt status if they function as lobbying arms.

Trade-off: Opponents will cite academic freedom. But disclosure isn't censorship—it's clarity. Voters deserve to know who's writing the footnotes.

VI. Conclusion: The Window Can Be Reopened

America doesn't suffer from a lack of opinions. It suffers from a lack of options.

Our political discourse feels toxic because it's being squeezed from all sides—by media consolidation that filters out real alternatives, by social platforms that addict us to outrage, and by think tanks that elevate elite preferences as expert consensus.

Together, these forces narrow the Overton window so effectively that even talking about structural reform feels naive or fringe.

It's not.

The first step toward reform is seeing how the system works—not just who shouts the loudest, but who gets heard at all. From there, we can begin to rebuild an information ecosystem that informs rather than manipulates, and a democracy where what's "possible" isn't defined by a handful of CEOs, billionaires, or backend code.

Truth is out there. But someone has to fight for it to be heard.

The Rise and Fall of the Fairness Doctrine — and Why Rebuilding It Today Would Almost Certainly Fail

From Equal Time to Echo Chambers

I. The Origins of the Fairness Doctrine

In 1949, the Federal Communications Commission (FCC) put the Fairness Doctrine into place. It was pretty simple at its core: if you had a license to broadcast over the public airwaves — whether radio or TV — you had two responsibilities. First, you had to devote airtime to important public issues. Second, you had to make a reasonable effort to present opposing viewpoints.

This wasn't seen as government censorship. Quite the opposite. At the time, there were only so many broadcast frequencies to go around. Airwaves were considered public property, and license holders were stewards, not owners. The Doctrine was framed as a constitutional compromise: instead of the government controlling content, broadcasters had a duty to cover a range of views fairly.

Between the 1950s and 1970s, the Fairness Doctrine helped

shape a media environment where extreme views got less traction. It didn't demand perfect balance, and it didn't require every broadcast to include every side. It simply leaned on broadcasters to make a genuine effort at honesty and diversity in public discourse.

II. The Death of the Doctrine

By the 1980s, that media landscape had cracked wide open. Cable television was booming. FM radio had exploded. New technologies, including early satellite communications, added even more ways to reach audiences. Scarcity was no longer the rule.

Meanwhile, the Reagan administration launched a broad deregulatory push across industries — energy, finance, telecommunications — and the media were no exception. Critics of the Fairness Doctrine argued that it actually suppressed speech. Stations, worried about triggering enforcement actions, often avoided controversial topics altogether. Better to say nothing than risk saying something "unbalanced."

In 1987, the FCC officially killed the Doctrine, declaring it outdated and unconstitutional. Congress tried to bring it back, but Reagan vetoed the effort.

The courts had already started laying the groundwork for this shift. In *Miami Herald Publishing Co. v. Tornillo* (1974), the Supreme Court struck down a Florida law that tried to force newspapers to publish political replies. The Court's ruling emphasized editorial discretion — the right of media outlets to decide for themselves what to publish. While *Tornillo* didn't directly apply to broadcasters (because of differences in how radio and television were regulated), the logic was clear: government-mandated editorial balance was on shaky constitutional ground.

Once the Fairness Doctrine was gone, talk radio — particularly conservative talk — exploded almost overnight. Rush Limbaugh's rise wasn't a fluke. It was a structural shift made possible by deregulation.

III. How Its Absence Shaped the Current Media Landscape

Without the Fairness Doctrine, media companies were free to pursue purely ideological programming. And they did — because it made money.

AM radio, which had been on life support in the early 1980s, found a new lease on life by going all-in on political talk. Conservative hosts dominated, not because of some conspiracy, but because their shows pulled loyal, engaged audiences — exactly what advertisers wanted.

Cable news channels followed the same logic. Rather than trying to appeal to a broad middle, networks realized it was more profitable to serve ideological niches. You didn't need everyone to watch — you just needed a loyal base who would tune in night after night.

The internet amplified this trend even further. Platforms like Facebook, YouTube, and Twitter (now X) allowed anyone to publish anything, anytime. Algorithms — automated systems that sort and recommend content — didn't prioritize balance. They prioritized engagement. If an angry, emotional headline got more clicks, it rose to the top, no matter how misleading it was.

The result was fragmentation on a scale that would have been unimaginable in the 1950s. Americans now live inside self-curated media ecosystems, increasingly isolated from opposing views.

IV. The Broader Effects on Politics and Culture

The collapse of shared media standards didn't just change what Americans watched. It changed how American politics works.

Politicians no longer have to moderate their views for mass audiences. Instead, they tailor their messages to hyper-specific ideological factions. Outrage isn't a byproduct anymore — it's the product.

Conspiracy theories, once relegated to crank pamphlets and late-night radio, now find mainstream audiences. Trust in major institutions — media, government, science — has collapsed because there's no longer a common frame of reference.

Meanwhile, basic media literacy — the ability to tell news from opinion, fact from spin — has eroded badly. Many people can't distinguish between a commentator venting and a reporter presenting verifiable information.

Debates that once revolved around a loosely agreed set of facts now spiral into separate realities. Arguments about elections, vaccines, economics — even physical reality itself — break down along tribal lines.

V. Why Rebuilding It Today Would Likely Fail

Could we resurrect something like the Fairness Doctrine? Technically, maybe. Practically, almost certainly not. Here's why:

- **First Amendment Law:** Courts today treat editorial control as a sacrosanct right. Forcing private companies to present opposing views would almost certainly be struck down as unconstitutional under current doctrine.

- **Decentralized Media:** The 1949 media world had three TV networks and a few dozen major radio stations. Today, there are millions of content outlets. Regulating them all would be logistically impossible.

- **Business Models:** Outrage sells. Tribal loyalty sells. Media companies and tech platforms have every financial reason to deepen ideological divides, not bridge them.

- **Public Distrust:** Any major government attempt to regulate media today would be immediately branded as censorship by one side or the other — and half the country would believe it.

Even softer measures — like requiring platforms to offer algorithmic transparency or user opt-outs — would face enormous pushback.

VI. Meaningful Changes That Could Still Work

While the Fairness Doctrine itself is dead and buried, some reforms could help mitigate the damage:

- **Transparency Laws:** Force platforms to reveal how their algorithms prioritize content, and whether they're amplifying certain types of information disproportionately.

- **Media Literacy in Schools:** Teach critical media analysis as a core subject, starting in elementary school and continuing through high school.

- **Algorithmic Opt-Outs:** Legally require social media platforms to let users see content in simple chronological order if they choose.

- **Public Funding for Journalism:** Fund nonprofit investigative journalism and local news through independent grants, insulated from direct political control.

- **Civic Content Pools:** Offer voluntary, curated collections of fact-based civic information that platforms can plug into their systems for free.

None of these would recreate a neutral media environment. But together, they could help slow the descent into complete epistemic chaos.

VII. How Remedies Would Be Attacked and Neutralized

Any serious media reform effort would face a predictable five-step attack plan:

1. **Frame it as censorship:** Claim that transparency or fairness rules are a stealth attack on free speech.

2. **Exploit technical complexity:** Argue that regulating algorithms is impossible or too dangerous to attempt.

3. **Stoke partisanship:** Paint reforms as a partisan plot to silence "the other side."

4. **Delay endlessly:** Use lawsuits, lobbying, and bureaucratic hurdles to bog reforms down until they quietly die.

5. **Co-opt regulators:** Capture and weaken enforcement bodies through corporate lobbying and strategic funding.

The endgame for any serious media reform proposal, if history is any guide, would be death by a thousand cuts.

VIII. The Future We Can Expect

Barring some fundamental cultural shift, here's the likely

future:

- Polarization will deepen.

- Americans will inhabit increasingly divergent realities.

- Algorithmic systems will grow more powerful and less transparent.

- "Truth" will become a market commodity, selected for emotional resonance rather than factual accuracy.

- Every major crisis — pandemics, elections, economic collapses — will trigger temporary demands for reform, but nothing lasting.

Without a radical reinvention of how Americans think about information and civic responsibility, informational fragmentation will continue — probably getting worse.

IX. Conclusion: The Dream and the Reality

The Fairness Doctrine was built for a world that barely exists anymore. It assumed a handful of broadcasters, a public sense of shared responsibility, and a basic belief in facts as the common ground for debate.

None of that holds true today.

While it's tempting to dream about rebuilding some kind of media fairness system, the reality is harder. You would need to rewrite constitutional law, restructure entire business models, rebuild shattered public trust, and redesign the technological architecture of communication itself.

None of those things are on the horizon.

The Fairness Doctrine is dead.

The world that made it possible is dead.

And no serious revival is coming.

Who Gets to Speak?

Gatekeeping, Platforms, and the Performance of Truth

Free speech is one of the most celebrated values in American democracy. But speech isn't power. Access is.

While digital platforms appear to democratize speech—allowing anyone to post or publish—the reality is more controlled than it seems. Through algorithms, elite institutions, and narrative framing, access to voice is tightly regulated. And in a system optimized for outrage, truth struggles to compete with content designed to provoke.

The stakes are real: Without reform, gatekeeping stifles democratic renewal by silencing critical voices. What matters isn't just who speaks—it's who gets heard, and who decides.

I. The Myth of the Open Marketplace

We often imagine public discourse as a "marketplace of ideas"—where the strongest arguments rise naturally. But in reality, modern marketplaces reward attention, not accuracy.

A 2018 MIT study found false information spreads six times faster than the truth on Twitter, largely because emotional content—fear, anger, shock—travels farther than calm analysis.

Platforms like YouTube, Facebook, and X (formerly Twitter) optimize content not for civic value, but for engagement. Their algorithms determine what's promoted, what's ignored, and what's quietly removed. In that system, even the best ideas get buried if they don't serve the profit model.

II. Platform Control Is the New Gatekeeping

Legacy gatekeepers—editors, publishers, network executives—once controlled who reached a public audience. Today, that control rests with private platform owners, moderation teams, and opaque algorithms.

After Elon Musk took over Twitter, policy changes triggered a measurable shift. The Center for Countering Digital Hate reported a 30% rise in hate speech, including a tripling of slurs targeting Black users.

The issue isn't Musk personally—it's structural. One person can now reshape global speech conditions without oversight or recourse. That's not a public square. It's a privatized megaphone.

III. The Performance of Speech vs. the Power of Voice

Speech and voice aren't the same.

- **Speech** is the ability to express an idea.
- **Voice** is being heard, taken seriously, and able to influence

outcomes.

Many people today can speak. Few have voice. They post, protest, or write—but are buried by systems that reward virality, not credibility.

Meanwhile, elite figures retain their voice even after failure. Pundits who supported the Iraq War still anchor shows. Financial executives who triggered economic collapse now advise policy. What matters isn't being right—it's being platform-compatible.

IV. Deplatforming, Cancellation, and Manufactured Victimhood

Deplatforming is real—but it often reinforces the very control it claims to challenge.

When content is removed without clear rules, users self-censor, unsure what crosses shifting lines. That chill doesn't just affect trolls—it discourages whistleblowers, reformers, and marginalized voices who lack institutional backing.

At the same time, those who shout loudest about being "canceled" often have the biggest platforms. What they're losing isn't speech—it's automatic legitimacy. The real silencing happens to people who never had a microphone in the first place.

V. Media and Institutional Exclusion

A. Media Framing and Distraction

Legacy media still sets the tone—and often narrows the scope—of national dialogue.

A 2020 study by Media Matters found that CNN devoted more coverage to polling and campaign drama than to economic policy, healthcare, or climate combined. Issues that define daily life were sidelined in favor of horse-race narratives.

The problem isn't censorship—it's agenda distortion. Complexity is flattened. Nuance is cut. Viewers are told who's winning, but not what's being debated.

B. Academic and Political Gatekeeping

Academic access remains tightly controlled:

- **Nature** charges over $11,000 to publish open-access research, locking out independent scholars.
- Public thinkers are often dismissed as unserious unless institutionally affiliated.
- Expertise is treated as valid only when filtered through elite pipelines.

In politics, influence skews toward wealth:

- In 2017, pharmaceutical lobbyists helped draft opioid

legislation, weakening DEA enforcement while sidelining public health experts.

- **OpenSecrets** data shows that donors consistently receive outsized access to lawmakers, while constituents wait in line.

Gatekeeping here isn't metaphorical—it's procedural.

VI. Narrative Control and the Boundaries of Imagination

The most effective censorship isn't banning ideas. It's deciding what counts as serious.

This boundary has a name: the Overton window—the range of ideas deemed acceptable in mainstream conversation. Anything outside it is dismissed as radical, naive, or unserious.

Examples:

- **Proportional representation**, used in New Zealand and over 90 other democracies, increased voter turnout by 5% after its adoption—but in the U.S., it's framed as unrealistic.

- **Universal healthcare**, despite broad popular support, is still treated as utopian rather than standard.

- **Participatory budgeting**, successfully implemented in New York and Paris, is ignored at the federal level—even though it measurably boosts civic trust.

When platforms and institutions define the limits of political imagination, democracy becomes performative—a structure that simulates change while suppressing alternatives.

VII. Real Reform Means Redesigning the System of Listening

Solving this isn't about mandating equal amplification. It's about rebuilding systems where influence reflects legitimacy—not reach.

Platform Reforms

- **Algorithmic transparency laws**: Let users see how decisions are made and challenge hidden biases in content promotion.

- **Federated platforms** (e.g., Mastodon): Built on protocols like **ActivityPub**, these systems allow users to host their own communities and escape centralized control.

- **Public-interest platforms**: Modeled on NPR or PBS, they could elevate underrepresented voices without profit pressure.

Civic and Institutional Reforms

- **Participatory journalism**: Programs like *City Bureau's Documenters* train and pay residents to cover local government. In Chicago, this model boosted meeting attendance by over 20%, increasing accountability from the ground up.

- **Citizen assemblies and juries**: Let random, demographically representative groups review laws or budgets—restoring democratic deliberation.
- **Expanded whistleblower protections**: Enable truth-tellers to speak safely and be heard.
- **Media literacy education**: Equip students to recognize manipulation and seek credible sources.

These are not theoretical. They are **already working**—just not yet at scale.

VIII. Conclusion: The Right to Speak is Foundational

We've built a society where almost anyone can talk—but only a few are allowed to matter.

If democracy is supposed to represent the people, then it can't afford to filter voice through wealth, performance, or algorithmic preference.

But the right to be heard—that's where reform begins.

When the Truth Stopped Mattering: How Free Societies and Dictatorships Both Killed Their Own Media

America's press hollowed itself out. Germany's press was crushed. Both left their people defenseless.

I. Style over Substance

Today, the American news media appears trapped in an endless cycle of triviality. Outrage erupts over the color of a president's suit, a misstep on a stairway, a word choice at a press conference. News coverage devotes disproportionate time to gaffes, optics, and fleeting moments, while matters of governance, systemic decay, and the mechanics of power barely register beyond specialized audiences. This phenomenon is often treated as if it were inevitable, a byproduct of living in a fast-moving, technologically advanced, and entertainment-saturated society. That assumption is false.

Historically, the collapse of serious media has been a marker of societal decline, not a natural feature of modernity. The American media's transformation was not random. It followed a clear, identifiable path: a shift from watchdog journalism to spectacle-driven entertainment. The corrosion of substance did not arise from external force but from internal decay — market incentives, technological changes, and public appetite converged to reward trivia over truth.

In stark contrast, regimes like Nazi Germany destroyed their media ecosystems through direct violence and totalitarian control. The Weimar Republic, for all its political instability, had a free press that exposed abuses and warned of extremism. That freedom was extinguished in months once Hitler seized power. The German public's access to truth was not eroded by trivialization; it was crushed under boot and decree.

Despite the radically different methods, both systems produced the same devastating result: a public stripped of its ability to understand, reason about, or meaningfully respond to the exercise of power. In both cases, media institutions ceased to perform their primary civic function. Whether through soft collapse or hard suppression, the death of serious news preceded the weakening of democratic culture.

This chapter traces these two distinct but converging paths: how the American press hollowed itself out through the trivial pursuits of spectacle, and how Germany's media was murdered outright by authoritarian force. Along the way, it will explore how Germany's postwar reconstruction offers critical lessons that America is now ignoring, and why a free press is necessary but not sufficient to preserve a functioning democracy.

Understanding this history is not merely an academic exercise. It is a roadmap for recognizing what happens when truth ceases to matter — and what may follow if the decay is not arrested.

II. Watergate and the 1970s — Peak of Investigative Journalism

In the 1970s, American journalism reached its modern high point. The function of the press as a check on political power was not simply theoretical; it was exercised with discipline and courage. The most iconic example of this era, the Watergate scandal, began not with a grand conspiracy but with a small crime: the burglary of the Democratic National Committee headquarters at the Watergate complex in Washington, D.C., in 1972.

What transformed that burglary into a constitutional crisis was the persistence of two reporters at *The Washington Post*, Bob Woodward and Carl Bernstein. Through months of meticulous investigation, they uncovered a network of illegal activity tied directly to the Nixon White House. Their work, initially dismissed by political insiders, ultimately revealed a systematic abuse of presidential power. The resulting scandal led to the first and only resignation of an American president.

The Watergate coverage was not an isolated event. It reflected a broader journalistic culture that rewarded seriousness. Editors invested in long, expensive investigations. Readers and viewers expected news outlets to confront those in power, not flatter them. Journalism operated, albeit imperfectly, as a public service rather than a branch of entertainment.

Critically, the media of this era understood that its credibility depended not on speed or spectacle, but on verification and thoroughness. When *The Washington Post* published new Watergate revelations, they were painstakingly sourced. Anonymous informants, such as the now-famous "Deep Throat," were corroborated before allegations were printed. Standards of evidence were central, not secondary, to reporting.

This environment was not perfect. American media had its blind spots and biases even then. However, the prevailing ethos was clear: the press existed to inform the public, hold the powerful accountable, and safeguard democratic norms. Success was measured by accuracy and public impact, not by engagement metrics or click rates.

Watergate demonstrated the essential role of a free, serious press. It also sowed the seeds of its future undoing. The visibility and prestige earned by investigative journalism in the 1970s transformed journalists into public figures and celebrities. With that transformation came new incentives: not merely to uncover the truth, but to be seen uncovering it. The subtle shift from journalism as a public duty to journalism as a personal platform began here, even if its full consequences would not manifest until decades later.

III. Reagan and the 1980s — Media's Shift Toward Optics

The election of Ronald Reagan in 1980 marked a profound shift in the relationship between American politics and the media. Reagan, a former Hollywood actor, understood the power of image better than any of his predecessors. He recognized that in an increasingly television-dominated landscape, how things looked often mattered more than what was actually said or done.

Reagan's presidency was meticulously stage-managed. Public appearances were choreographed down to minor details: lighting, backdrops, camera angles. Speeches were saturated with optimistic, cinematic imagery — "Morning in America" became not just a campaign slogan but a governing philosophy of constant emotional uplift. Policy discussions were reframed as narratives of hope and destiny rather than deliberations about costs and consequences.

The press initially tried to resist this shift. Many reporters recognized that Reagan's administration was using stagecraft to divert attention from complex or controversial policies. However, television news, by its nature, found it easier and more profitable to broadcast stirring visuals and simple soundbites than to conduct deep policy analysis.

This was not merely laziness or conspiracy. The medium itself — television — privileged immediacy, emotional resonance, and visual storytelling. A compelling image of Reagan speaking before a flag-draped backdrop traveled farther and faster than a lengthy analysis of deregulation or military spending. Audiences responded positively to the uplifting imagery and accessible narratives. In turn, media outlets, driven by ratings pressures, adapted their coverage to focus more heavily on optics.

The subtle but critical change was that style began to rival substance as a political currency. It became increasingly difficult for journalists to generate sustained public interest in detailed policy critiques when soaring rhetoric and appealing images captured emotional loyalty more efficiently. Coverage shifted from asking "What is happening?" to "How does it look?" and "How will it play?"

This transformation laid the groundwork for the future trivialization of news. If appearances mattered as much as, or more than, actions, then political journalism inevitably drifted toward focusing on the ephemeral: gestures, wardrobe choices, facial expressions, gaffes. Reagan did not create this dynamic intentionally as a scheme to erode journalism; he simply understood, better than his opponents and even much of the press, how to thrive in a media environment where the appearance of success could shield the exercise of power from serious scrutiny.

By the end of the 1980s, American political journalism had been permanently altered. It had not yet abandoned its public service ideals entirely, but it was increasingly operating under incentives that rewarded presentation over substance. The structure of news had begun shifting toward what would become its defining characteristic decades later: a focus on what was visually arresting, emotionally resonant, and easy to consume — even if it was substantively hollow.

IV. Clinton and the 1990s — The Tabloidization of American News

By the 1990s, the American media environment had undergone a fundamental transformation. The technological landscape now included 24-hour cable news channels, most notably CNN, founded in 1980 but reaching full dominance in the new decade. The economic model of journalism was shifting rapidly: attention, not merely accuracy or depth, became the primary currency. News organizations had to fill airtime continuously, competing not just with each other but with emerging entertainment options for audience retention.

The presidency of Bill Clinton collided directly with this evolving media ecosystem. Clinton, young, charismatic, and vulnerable to personal scandal, became an ideal subject for the new media incentives. His administration's policies — welfare reform, financial deregulation, healthcare efforts — were complex and often demanded serious, nuanced coverage. But it was personal scandal that offered far more profitable content.

The Gennifer Flowers affair allegations during the 1992 campaign foreshadowed the era to come. By the time of the Monica Lewinsky scandal in 1998, the transition was complete. Major networks, newspapers, and newly rising internet platforms devoted months of continuous coverage to the president's personal misconduct. The actual constitutional issues at stake — perjury, obstruction of justice, separation of powers — were often buried under endless, prurient speculation about dress stains, taped conversations, and intimate details of private encounters.

Two structural shifts locked this tabloidization into place:

- Economic incentives: Scandal coverage delivered consistently high ratings and traffic.

- Technological pressure: 24-hour news cycles demanded perpetual novelty, even when real events did not justify it.

Substance became increasingly difficult to sustain under these conditions. In-depth policy reporting was expensive, time-consuming, and less immediately rewarding. Covering the latest twist in a sex scandal, by contrast, was cheap, fast, and guaranteed to drive public interest. Even once-serious outlets adapted: *The New York Times*, *The Washington Post*, and network news all devoted front pages and lead stories to minute developments in the Lewinsky affair.

This was a critical break from the Watergate-era ethos. In the 1970s, journalists investigated misconduct to illuminate abuses of power. In the 1990s, journalists increasingly investigated personal scandal for its entertainment value, often treating political coverage as a branch of celebrity gossip.

It is important to be clear: It was not that scandals had no legitimate public importance. The president's conduct, honesty, and respect for the law matter in a democracy. But the media's obsessive, sensationalized framing of those scandals detached them from serious civic discussion. Scandals became soap operas, with heroes, villains, cliffhangers, and endless "breaking news" alerts, regardless of substance.

By the end of the 1990s, the American press had largely completed its transition: from a Fourth Estate dedicated to public accountability, to an entertainment complex locked in competition for scandal, spectacle, and speed.

V. Bush and the 2000s — Patriotism, Deference, and the Death of Critical Coverage

The early 2000s delivered a shock to the American media system that at first appeared to offer an opportunity for seriousness to reassert itself. The terrorist attacks of September 11, 2001, thrust politics, governance, and national security back to the forefront of public life. For a brief moment, the country seemed to demand factual, sober reporting rather than triviality.

But the reality was different. The trauma of 9/11 created an overwhelming wave of patriotic unity, and within that environment, critical journalism became not just unfashionable but stigmatized as unpatriotic. The administration of George W. Bush understood and exploited this atmosphere. Complex policy debates about surveillance powers, civil liberties, and foreign intervention were drowned under simple slogans: "You are either with us or against us."

The media, still adapting to the 24-hour news cycle and increasingly risk-averse about alienating audiences, largely capitulated. Journalistic institutions that had once prided themselves on skepticism treated official government claims with unwarranted deference. Nowhere was this more visible than in the lead-up to the Iraq War.

From late 2002 through early 2003, major American news outlets amplified government assertions about weapons of mass destruction (WMDs) in Iraq with minimal independent verification. The *New York Times*, among others, published front-page stories that lent credibility to unfounded intelligence claims. Television news, especially cable outlets like CNN and Fox News, often treated official press conferences and anonymous leaks as primary reporting rather than starting points for investigation.

The consequences were severe. The American public, relying on a media system that had historically acted as a check on government narratives, was misled about the necessity and urgency of a war. Later investigations revealed that critical voices inside the intelligence community were marginalized, that evidentiary standards were grossly compromised, and that the press had failed in its watchdog function at precisely the moment it was most needed.

At the same time, election coverage evolved further into horse-race journalism — political reporting that treats campaigns like sporting events. Rather than focusing on candidates' policies, platforms, or records, media coverage emphasized polling numbers, fundraising totals, debate "zingers," and momentary shifts in "momentum." The analytical frame became "Who's winning?" rather than "What does this mean for the governed?"

Two dynamics worked in parallel:
- In foreign affairs and national security, patriotic deference

replaced critical journalism.

- In domestic politics, horse-race coverage replaced substantive analysis.

Both trends fed the public's growing detachment from serious engagement with governance. News became a mixture of rallying cries and scorekeeping, rather than a forum for civic education.

Importantly, this was not solely the fault of government manipulation. It was also a failure of journalistic institutions, which chose to prioritize fear of alienating their audiences over the professional risk of speaking inconvenient truths.

By the end of the Bush era, the American media had suffered not just from market pressures toward entertainment but from a deep internal crisis of mission. It had been shown that when fear and nationalism rose, much of the supposedly independent press could be counted on to abandon skepticism and investigative rigor without a single shot being fired at them.

VI. Obama and the 2010s — The Outrage Click Economy

The election of Barack Obama in 2008 initially sparked hopes that American political journalism might recover its seriousness. Obama, a former constitutional law professor, engaged in policy-heavy campaigns that emphasized healthcare reform, financial regulation, and restoring America's standing abroad. For a time, there was a resurgence of detailed political reporting, especially during the 2008 financial crisis.

However, the structural pressures driving media trivialization had not disappeared. They had, in fact, accelerated with the rise of social media platforms — particularly Facebook (founded 2004), Twitter (founded 2006), and later Instagram (founded 2010). These platforms rewired how news was consumed: audiences now encountered news stories primarily through shares, likes, and emotionally charged headlines rather than direct subscriptions or newsstand purchases.

The fundamental business model of journalism shifted again. Clicks became king. Advertising revenue no longer flowed predictably to newspapers or nightly newscasts; it was tied to digital engagement. Content that triggered strong emotional reactions — anger, outrage, indignation — spread farther and faster than content that demanded contemplation or conveyed nuance.

American media outlets, desperate to survive financially, adapted. They learned to optimize headlines for outrage and to frame stories in ways that would generate maximum emotional engagement. Outrage was not simply a byproduct of news coverage — it became a core feature of the product itself.

Against this backdrop, Obama's presidency was covered

increasingly through trivial, optics-obsessed lenses. Complex policy debates, such as the negotiation of the Affordable Care Act or the Iran nuclear deal, struggled for airtime against far more superficial controversies.

Among the most infamous examples:

- The "tan suit" scandal in August 2014, when Obama wore a light-colored suit during a press conference about foreign policy.

- The "latte salute" controversy in September 2014, when Obama saluted Marines while holding a coffee cup in the same hand.

These incidents were not, in themselves, significant. They were manufactured scandals — non-events elevated to national attention because they fit the new media economy's need for outrage and easy clicks.

Meanwhile, serious governance stories — Obama's expansion of drone warfare, mass surveillance revelations, structural economic inequality — received far less sustained coverage. These topics were harder to package into viral headlines or quick emotional appeals.

The lesson American media had internalized by the end of the 2010s was simple: In the competition for survival, it was safer and more profitable to cover the politics of optics, scandal, and outrage than the complexities of governance.

This shift did not merely degrade public understanding; it rewired the expectations of the audience itself. Citizens came to expect that political engagement would be mediated through constant emotional provocation rather than rational deliberation. Journalism increasingly resembled entertainment not just in format, but in function.

VII. Trump and the 2015–2025 Era — Politics as Entertainment

If the Reagan presidency taught the media the importance of optics, and the Obama era solidified the dominance of the outrage economy, the rise of Donald Trump completed the transformation of American political journalism into pure entertainment.

Trump, a longtime New York real estate magnate and reality television star, understood instinctively what many political professionals and journalists had only dimly perceived: in the new media ecosystem, attention was power, and outrage was the most reliable engine of attention. He did not merely adapt to the media environment — he weaponized it.

From the moment Trump descended the golden escalator at Trump Tower in June 2015 to announce his candidacy, his every move was crafted to dominate coverage. Outlandish statements, personal insults, and shocking provocations were not gaffes or missteps; they were deliberate strategies to command the media's focus.

The traditional gatekeeping role of journalism — the idea that editors and producers could determine which stories were "important" — collapsed almost immediately. Trump's ability to generate ratings was too lucrative to resist. News outlets, even those openly critical of Trump, found themselves devoting massive amounts of airtime to his rallies, tweets, and controversies, often live-broadcasting events that offered no substantive policy discussion.

Two dynamics accelerated the collapse of serious political journalism:

- **Total attention capture:** Trump's unpredictability made him impossible to ignore.
- **Audience addiction to outrage:** After a decade of conditioning, audiences expected political news to deliver continuous emotional stimulation.

Journalists themselves, many of whom despised Trump personally, were caught in a self-defeating cycle. Criticism, fact-checking, and analysis were all performed — often with real rigor — but the sheer volume of coverage centered Trump in the national consciousness every hour of every day. He was inescapable.

Serious issues — healthcare policy, regulatory changes, foreign diplomacy, judicial appointments — were often buried beneath the flood of scandal coverage, Twitter feuds, and palace intrigue. Trump's governance style blurred entertainment and statecraft to such a degree that even informed citizens struggled to separate spectacle from substance.

Importantly, Trump's success in dominating media coverage revealed rather than caused the systemic weakness of American journalism. The structures built during decades of prioritizing spectacle over substance, personality over policy, and outrage over investigation made it impossible for the press to reassert control once it mattered most.

By the time of the 2020 and 2024 elections, political coverage often resembled celebrity gossip more than civic reporting. Investigative journalism persisted, often performing heroically under difficult conditions, but it was drowned out by the sheer volume of attention dedicated to daily outrage and performative conflict.

Thus, by 2025, American media had fully completed its journey:

- From watchdog to spectacle curator.
- From Fourth Estate to Fourth Ring in a circus.

It had not been crushed by force, as in Nazi Germany. It had been hollowed out by its own internal weaknesses — amplified by new technology, market incentives, and public appetite for endless drama.

VIII. Result — American Media Hollowed Out by Its Own Freedom

By the middle of the 2020s, the American media system stood hollowed, not by external censorship or authoritarian decree, but by its own internal evolution. The very freedoms that once empowered the press to act as a guardian of democracy had, without structural protections or cultural discipline, been weaponized against its foundational purpose.

Unlike in totalitarian regimes, where journalism is destroyed at gunpoint, the American media hollowed itself willingly, incentivized by market forces, technological changes, and a public that gradually came to expect outrage and spectacle instead of investigation and analysis.

Each stage of the decline built logically upon the last:

- From Watergate's disciplined scrutiny to Reagan's dominance of optics,
- From Clinton's tabloidization to Bush's patriotic deference,
- From Obama's clickbait economy to Trump's total

spectacle,

- Each decade accelerated the shift away from serious engagement with governance.

The underlying causes were structural, not simply the fault of bad individuals. The economic collapse of traditional journalism funding models — classified ads, subscriptions, and reliable television ad revenue — created desperate competition for attention. Social media platforms monetized emotional outrage more efficiently than reasoned argument. Newsrooms, stripped of resources, increasingly followed the path of least resistance: chasing controversy, provoking anger, sustaining endless superficial conflicts to keep audiences emotionally engaged.

What was lost was not merely "better journalism." What was lost was the public's ability to meaningfully reason about power.

When news is reduced to optics, scandals, and emotional spectacle, citizens cannot properly understand how laws are made, how policies are enacted, how rights are eroded, or how institutions are corrupted. They may feel constantly stimulated by news consumption, but they are left disoriented — angry without clear understanding, cynical without clear alternatives, exhausted without clear knowledge.

This outcome is, in some ways, more dangerous than overt

censorship. In authoritarian regimes, the suppression of truth is visible, concrete, and sometimes possible to resist through underground information networks. In a spectacle-driven democracy, the collapse of truth is hidden beneath a flood of endless information, much of it trivial or emotionally manipulative. Citizens believe they are informed because they are saturated with news content, even as their real understanding of governance deteriorates.

By the mid-2020s, the American public was not merely uninformed about key aspects of policy and governance — it was systematically miseducated by a media economy optimized for emotional spectacle. The ability of the electorate to act as a check on power weakened accordingly, not because information was inaccessible, but because information had been devalued, obscured, and replaced with endless drama.

This was not a temporary deviation. It represented a structural failure: a free press that forgot freedom requires seriousness to survive. Without a culture that values truth over entertainment, and without institutions designed to prioritize substance over spectacle, even the freest press can become functionally useless.

IX. Germany — Destruction of the Free Press by Force

While American media collapsed through internal decay,

the destruction of the German free press during the rise of Adolf Hitler followed a very different path — one of direct, violent suppression. Yet the ultimate result was strikingly similar: a public stripped of reliable, independent access to truth.

In the final years of the Weimar Republic (1918–1933), Germany's media was vibrant but chaotic. There were hundreds of newspapers representing every political stripe: liberal, conservative, socialist, communist, nationalist. The press covered Adolf Hitler's rise aggressively. Major newspapers reported on Nazi street violence, Hitler's inflammatory rhetoric, and the anti-democratic aims of the National Socialist German Workers' Party (NSDAP).

Journalists did not fail to warn the public. What failed was the public's willingness to act on those warnings. Economic despair, political fragmentation, and national humiliation after World War I left many Germans susceptible to radical solutions, regardless of media exposure to the dangers.

When Hitler was appointed Chancellor in January 1933, the transition from contested politics to dictatorship was rapid. The pivotal moment came one month later, with the Reichstag Fire on February 27, 1933. A Dutch communist was arrested for the arson, but the Nazi leadership seized the event as a pretext to crush civil liberties.

The next day, Hitler invoked Article 48 of the Weimar Constitution, which allowed for emergency decrees. The Reichstag Fire Decree suspended freedom of speech, freedom of the press, freedom of assembly, and constitutional protections against arbitrary detention. It enabled the police to arrest political opponents without judicial oversight and to ban newspapers deemed "threatening to public security."

Within weeks, Germany's free press was effectively dead. The process of Gleichschaltung — meaning "coordination" — forcibly aligned all independent institutions, including the media, with Nazi ideology. Newspapers were either shut down, violently intimidated into compliance, or absorbed into the centralized propaganda system. Opposition journalists were arrested, exiled, or killed.

By 1934, the independent German press no longer existed. In its place stood a vast propaganda machine managed by Joseph Goebbels' Ministry of Public Enlightenment and Propaganda. Every newspaper article, every radio broadcast, every public film was crafted to serve the regime's goals. Independent reporting, critical inquiry, and factual contradiction were eliminated by force.

The German public still received "news," but it was a hollowed version of reality: curated victories, mythologized leadership, and fabricated enemies. When dissent is not merely discredited but criminalized, truth itself becomes a form of resistance — and few are willing or able to resist under such conditions.

X. Germany Post-1945 — Controlled Reconstruction, Eventual Recovery

The collapse of Nazi Germany in May 1945 left behind not only physical ruins but also a media landscape utterly stripped of legitimacy and independence. The Allied powers — the United States, Britain, France, and the Soviet Union — recognized that rebuilding Germany would require more than political restructuring. It would require rebuilding an entirely new media culture from scratch.

The Allies understood that free press institutions would not simply regenerate themselves. After twelve years of totalitarian propaganda, the habits of independent journalism had been extinguished. As a result, they imposed direct control over all media operations in occupied Germany.

Every existing newspaper, radio station, and publishing house was shut down immediately upon Germany's surrender. No media institution that had survived under Nazi rule was allowed to continue. In their place, the Allied occupation authorities issued strict licenses for new newspapers and broadcast stations. Only Germans who could demonstrate a commitment to democratic values and a record free of Nazi collaboration were permitted to publish.

During the first phase of occupation (1945–1947), media operations were heavily censored and ideologically managed. Topics forbidden included:

- Promotion of militarism.
- Glorification of Nazi figures or ideology.
- Undermining the goals of the Allied Control Council.

At the same time, media outlets were encouraged — and often required — to promote values associated with liberal democracy: human rights, parliamentary governance, rule of law. Newspapers such as *Süddeutsche Zeitung* (Munich) and *Frankfurter Rundschau* (Frankfurt) were among the first licensed under these strict controls.

Importantly, factual reporting within approved boundaries was permitted and encouraged. Unlike Nazi propaganda, which had distorted or invented facts, Allied-licensed media was generally truthful about local events, reconstruction efforts, and political developments — provided those truths did not contradict Allied policy goals.

The goal was not to create a free press immediately, but to create the conditions in which a free press could eventually survive.

By 1947, as Cold War tensions escalated and as West Germany's provisional democratic institutions took shape, the Allied powers — particularly the United States and Britain — began relaxing their media control. German-run newspapers increasingly reported critically on issues like food shortages, black market activities, and administrative inefficiencies within the occupation zones.

1949 marked the decisive turning point. The founding of the Federal Republic of Germany (West Germany) brought full constitutional sovereignty and with it a legally protected free press. The Basic Law (Grundgesetz), West Germany's new constitution, guaranteed in Article 5:

- Freedom of speech.
- Freedom of the press.
- Freedom of broadcasting.

The licensing system was dismantled. Censorship powers were revoked. Journalists and media outlets were now free to operate independently, subject only to ordinary legal constraints such as libel laws.

Over the next two decades, West Germany developed one of the most respected and serious press environments in the world. Publications such as *Der Spiegel* and broadcasters like ARD and ZDF became models of investigative rigor and editorial independence.

By contrast, in Soviet-controlled East Germany, the media was rebuilt under totalitarian control. Newspapers and broadcasters were tightly subordinated to the Socialist Unity Party (SED). Press freedom did not exist; propaganda did.

The lesson is critical:

- Freedom of the press must be actively reconstructed after collapse.

- Structural protections must be built deliberately, not assumed.

- Cultural seriousness must be restored over time through practice and example.

Germany's postwar experience demonstrated that rebuilding serious journalism after catastrophic collapse is possible — but only with intentional institutional design, cultural commitment, and years of disciplined effort. Freedom alone, without structure and seriousness, would not have been enough.

XI. Comparison — Different Paths, Same Destination

When comparing the collapse of serious journalism in the United States and in Nazi Germany, it is critical to recognize that the mechanisms of destruction were diametrically opposed — yet the end result was functionally similar.

In Nazi Germany, the free press was destroyed by force. Constitutional protections were suspended. Independent journalists were silenced by decree, censorship, imprisonment, or death. Truth was criminalized, and public discourse was forcibly transformed into an instrument of state power. The press ceased to be a watchdog and became a megaphone for propaganda.

In the United States, the free press was hollowed out by freedom without structure. There were no decrees. No laws were passed banning serious journalism. No journalists were imprisoned for exposing uncomfortable facts. Instead, the collapse came through slow corrosion:

- Market forces rewarded triviality over substance.
- New technologies incentivized outrage over investigation.
- Cultural expectations shifted toward entertainment rather than civic education.

In both cases, the ultimate damage was the same: the public was deprived of meaningful, reliable information about how power was exercised.

In Nazi Germany, the collapse of truth was enforced through violent censorship and totalitarian control, unfolding rapidly between 1933 and 1934. In contrast, the United States experienced a slower erosion of truth from the 1970s to the 2020s, driven less by overt repression and more by market incentives and cultural decay. While Nazi propaganda replaced truth through fear and coercion, the American decline replaced truth with spectacle, leading not to fearful compliance but to widespread cynicism, disengagement, and confusion.

The contrast in methods obscures the deeper similarity in outcomes. In both societies, the press ceased to function as a check on power, and the citizenry's ability to reason about political life deteriorated.

Importantly, one system failed through the abuse of power; the other failed through the abdication of responsibility. Nazi Germany shows that a free press can be murdered by dictatorship. Modern America shows that a free press can commit suicide by trivialization.

Neither outcome was inevitable.

- In Germany, earlier and more forceful public resistance might have made Gleichschaltung more difficult.

- In America, a serious cultural commitment to structural press reforms, educational initiatives, and the defense of journalistic integrity might have slowed or reversed the decay.

But both systems illustrate a vital truth: press freedom alone is insufficient. It must be paired with cultural seriousness, institutional design, and public expectations that reward substance over spectacle. Otherwise, media institutions, whether crushed or corroded, will cease to serve the public good — and democracy will wither accordingly.

XII. Conclusion — Freedom Alone Is Not Enough

The collapse of serious journalism is not unique to any one time, place, or political system. It is a recurrent danger wherever media institutions fail to defend their core purpose: to provide the public with factual, substantive information about the exercise of power.

Nazi Germany destroyed its free press through brute force, extinguishing truth beneath censorship, imprisonment, and terror. Modern America hollowed out its press through the slow erosion of seriousness, substituting spectacle, scandal, and outrage for investigation, context, and understanding.

The methods differed. The final results did not.

- A public unable to reason about power.

- A press unable, or unwilling, to challenge that power meaningfully.

- A democracy weakened from within, before any external enemy could strike.

The common lesson is clear: Freedom alone does not guarantee a healthy press. Freedom must be paired with structural protections, economic models that reward substance, and a civic culture that values truth over entertainment. Without these supports, even the freest society can drift into informational collapse.

The reconstruction of West Germany's media after 1945 offers proof that serious journalism can be rebuilt. It requires intentional design, strict defense of press independence, and cultural reeducation about the role of truth in public life. It demands institutions that are more resilient than the passing whims of outrage and spectacle.

America today stands at a crossroads similar in importance, though different in form. The press has not been crushed. It has been compromised by its own pursuit of survival in a market that rewards emotional manipulation. Yet recovery remains possible — if, and only if, the public demands it, and if media institutions are willing to undergo painful, structural reforms that prioritize truth above clicks.

Otherwise, the fate is already visible. The death of serious media is not simply a media story. It is the prelude to the death of democratic governance itself.

When the truth stops mattering, freedom does not die with a bang.

It dies with a shrug — drowned in noise, spectacle, and the

comfortable lie that knowing everything is the same as understanding anything.

Protests Don't Work, Except When They Do

There's a Reason You Have to Get a Permit

Critics often argue that protests are largely performative and ineffective, claiming that public demonstrations rarely translate into concrete policy outcomes. From this perspective, protest is seen as emotional rather than strategic, a way to feel politically engaged without actually moving the levers of power. Demonstrators are accused of demanding simplistic solutions to complex problems and undermining the more serious work of legislation, legal reform, or electoral participation.

Another common critique focuses on disruption. Protests are said to create unnecessary chaos, strain law enforcement, block public services, and in some cases lead to property damage or looting. Opponents claim that such tactics alienate the public and reinforce political polarization, making it harder to reach consensus or enact reform. When any violence or vandalism occurs, critics often seize on these moments to delegitimize entire movements.

A longstanding accusation, particularly from far-right

media, is that many protesters are not genuinely motivated but are instead paid or organized by shadowy groups. This idea implies that the protests are inauthentic, astroturfed events rather than genuine expressions of public concern. Along with claims of virtue signaling and social media clout-chasing, this argument is meant to undermine the moral and civic legitimacy of protest itself.

While some protests are symbolic, they often serve as the initial catalyst for broader structural change. History shows that protest is not the final step in political reform but the first. Demonstrations increase public awareness, draw media attention, and apply pressure on institutions that might otherwise ignore emerging crises. Court cases and legislation do not emerge in isolation. They are frequently the result of sustained, disruptive, and visible movements that shift the public agenda.

The idea that protests are unproductive ignores the long list of reforms that began with people in the streets. For example:

- The Civil Rights Act of 1964
- The Voting Rights Act of 1965
- Women gaining the right to vote (19th Amendment)
- The end of the Vietnam War
- Marriage equality and the broader LGBTQ+ rights movement

- The creation of the Environmental Protection Agency
- The end of "Don't Ask, Don't Tell" in the military
- Stricter gun laws in some states after March for Our Lives
- Wage increases in multiple cities after the Fight for $15 campaign
- Abolition of child labor and establishment of the 8-hour workday
- Cancellation of the Keystone XL pipeline
- Expansion of AIDS treatment and research following ACT UP demonstrations
- Heightened police accountability measures following Black Lives Matter protests

These are not isolated examples. They span decades, demographics, and political contexts. The idea that protest does nothing collapses under the weight of American history.

Claims that protesters are paid actors are not new. Similar accusations were made during the civil rights era, the anti-war movement, and every major labor strike of the 20th century. These narratives are usually deployed to delegitimize public action without addressing the content of the protest itself. Suggesting that dissent must be compensated in order to exist is not only cynical, it is historically illiterate. People do not risk arrest or violence for a small paycheck. They do so because something is fundamentally wrong.

Disruption is not a failure of protest. It is the method by which it forces a response. Protests are designed to interrupt the status quo so that the issues at hand can no longer be ignored. A perfectly orderly and polite demonstration may be easier to tolerate, but it is also easier to dismiss. The discomfort protests create is a feature, not a flaw. It reflects the urgency of unresolved problems.

In the end, the claim that protests are useless is not a neutral observation. It is often a strategy to convince people not to resist. If protests were truly ineffective, the powerful would not spend so much time trying to prevent them.

Born Logged In: How a Hyperconnected Generation Is Rewriting the Political Script

What happens when the most online generation in history inherits a democracy they were never taught to navigate?

I. They've Never Known Disconnection

Most members of Gen Z—and the generation rising behind them—have never lived in a world that wasn't wired. There was no transition to digital life. They were born into it.

From the moment they could hold a device, they've absorbed language, norms, and politics through pixels. The internet wasn't something they adopted. It was the air.

This kind of immersion doesn't just change how people communicate. It changes how they think—what they believe is real, who they trust, and how they perceive power. And the way these young people are responding to political dysfunction is radically different from anything we've seen before.

II. Constant Exposure, Constant Judgment

For today's youth, everything is observed, recorded, and

commented on. A middle school hallway fight in the 1990s ended with a suspension or a paddling. Today it ends with a video, a hashtag, and a global audience.

Phones became mirrors, classrooms, stages, and battlegrounds. Image and performance were no longer optional—they were mandatory. Algorithms reward outrage, and young people learn early how to curate themselves into digestibility.

It's not just exhausting. It's formative. When identity is shaped under constant surveillance—by peers, platforms, and brands—critical thinking becomes both more urgent and more difficult.

III. The Education Gap: Curriculum vs. Reality

Most U.S. schools rely on outdated civics curricula, like those tied to Common Core, which emphasize memorizing government structures over understanding real-world power.

Students may learn how a bill becomes a law—but not how that bill gets gutted by lobbyists, buried in committee, or manipulated through procedural obstruction.

Some districts have introduced media literacy, but the programs are patchwork and underfunded. Most students still graduate without understanding how algorithms filter their feeds or how confirmation bias warps perception.

We've handed kids the equivalent of nuclear tools for narrative creation—and given them a pamphlet from 1985.

IV. Disinformation Targets the Distracted

It's not just that young people are online. It's that bad actors know they are—and design content accordingly.

On TikTok, influencer propaganda is dressed up as "hot takes." On YouTube, algorithmically boosted creators mimic progressive language while inserting fascist talking points. "Redpill" accounts on Instagram blend misogyny with meme aesthetics.

These tactics work because platforms are optimized for emotional reward. They exploit dopamine-driven engagement systems, where shock and identity validation consistently outperform nuance or fact.

For instance, during the 2020 election, a viral TikTok campaign claimed ballots in Georgia were being shredded—based on grainy footage of a recycling truck. The video reached millions before being debunked by state officials. By then, the damage was done.

Bad information doesn't need to convince everyone. It just needs to circulate faster than the correction.

V. But They're Not Buying It—Not All of It

Despite the noise, today's young people are not passive consumers.

This is the most pro-equality, pro-diversity, anti-authoritarian generation in decades. They're skeptical of institutions, but passionate about justice. They're not afraid to call out racism, homophobia, or hypocrisy—even when it's coming from the people who claim to represent them.

They speak in memes, move in swarms, and make culture faster than most politicians can draft a press release. They don't trust the system—but they haven't checked out either.

From organizing #BlackLivesMatter protests on Twitter to building turnout campaigns on Discord, Gen Z is already reshaping politics, even without institutional backing.

The challenge isn't apathy. It's fragmentation—and the lack of structural support for their civic instincts.

VI. What They're Missing—and What They Know

Many young people can't name their state representative. But they can explain how YouTube's algorithm pushes users toward conspiracy content.

They've grown up in an era of political spectacle—where truth is secondary to virality, and loyalty often outweighs logic.

They understand the game.

What they need is access to the rules that would let them shape it—on their terms.

Civics has failed them. But their instincts are sharp. They crave meaning, structure, and fairness. What they get is noise.

VII. Counterarguments—and Why They Miss the Mark
"Gen Z is just apathetic."

→ Far from it. Gen Z drove record youth turnout in the 2020 and 2022 elections and powers movements like March for Our Lives, Fridays for Future, and unionization drives at places like Starbucks. Their engagement is real—it's just not always filtered through traditional channels.

"Traditional civics is enough."

→ Memorizing government branches doesn't equip students to navigate algorithm-driven disinformation, weaponized polarization, or modern suppression tactics. Civic knowledge without digital fluency is like learning to read without ever seeing a book.

"They're too distracted for serious politics."

→ Gen Z grew up multitasking across apps, formats, and conversations. They're not distracted—they're distributed. Many use that fluency to mobilize, fundraise, and inform peers across multiple platforms at once. What looks like distraction is often decentralized organizing.

VIII. Reform Means Partnering with the Already Awake

Reform doesn't mean preaching to young people. It means resourcing them. Partnering with them. Trusting that their instincts—when sharpened—can change everything.

Reform starts with foundational media literacy: training students (and each other) to spot bias, trace funding, and recognize algorithmic framing.

Civics must evolve to reflect actual power: how legislation gets blocked, how narratives are shaped, and who profits from disengagement.

We need platform accountability: mandating transparency in recommendation systems like YouTube's and TikTok's, and regulating algorithm design so accuracy isn't penalized by the system itself.

We need federal support for peer-led initiatives: youth-created civic apps, school-based civic media projects, and funding for Gen Z-run advocacy orgs working to rebuild democratic trust from the ground up.

We already have examples. California's 2024 media literacy law mandates digital literacy in K–12 classrooms. The News Literacy Project gives teachers and students tools to decode disinformation. The Poor People's Campaign mobilizes multi-faith, multi-racial youth coalitions around justice and democratic renewal.

Now scale them. Fund them. Pair them with algorithmic reform and cultural legitimacy.

IX. Conclusion: The Future's Already Online
Reforming democracy means adapting to the generation inheriting it. Not condescending to them. Not romanticizing them. But meeting them where they are—with humility, honesty, and infrastructure.

They don't need to be told what to think. They need tools to sharpen the clarity they already bring. Because if we don't help them see how power works, someone else will. And that someone probably isn't interested in democracy.

The Quiet Coup: How Capital Beat Labor, One Law at a Time

Wealth today is not just accumulated. It is fortified.

I. How the Rich Changed the Rules — and the Story About the Rules

Most people sense something is wrong with the way money moves today. They can feel the growing gap between the wealthy and everyone else, even if they cannot always articulate how it happened. Some blame globalization. Others blame technology. But underneath those forces runs a quieter, older story: the rules were changed.

The last half-century in America has been defined by two quiet revolutions. The first was a structural rewiring of the tax system that allowed capital to escape taxation while labor remained exposed. The second was a consolidation of media power that shaped how the public understood — or more often misunderstood — what was happening. Together, they built a system where wealth not only accumulates but becomes nearly impossible to dislodge.

This is the story of how the rich lowered their taxes, preserved their gains, and controlled the narrative about both.

II. The Golden Age of High Taxes and Low Inequality

In the aftermath of World War II, the United States operated under a set of economic rules that would seem almost alien today. The top federal income tax rate was 91 percent. It applied to the portion of income above what would be about two million dollars a year in today's terms. Corporate tax rates hovered around 50 percent. Capital gains were taxed at 25 percent.

Far from strangling the economy, the 1950s and early 1960s were periods of broad-based prosperity. Wages grew in lockstep with productivity. Wealth inequality, which had been extreme in the early 20th century, was at historic lows. Most Americans lived in a world where a single income could support a family, buy a house, and fund a retirement.

The wealthy still lived well. Private jets existed. Mansions stood. But structurally, the system demanded that high income meant high contribution. The idea that billionaires would one day pay lower effective tax rates than nurses or teachers would have been seen as absurd.

III. Breaking the Gold Standard and Breaking Public Patience

The first cracks began not with taxes but with money itself.

In 1971, President Nixon took the United States off the Bretton Woods gold standard. Until then, the dollar was theoretically convertible to gold at a fixed rate. In practice, foreign governments could demand gold in exchange for dollars, anchoring the currency to a physical asset. With mounting trade deficits, rising debt, and inflationary pressure, Nixon severed the link.

Once the gold window closed, the U.S. dollar became a fiat currency, backed only by government promise. Almost immediately, inflation accelerated. Prices rose, sometimes dramatically. But the tax system had not adjusted. Federal income tax brackets were fixed, not indexed to inflation. As wages rose nominally to keep pace with prices, Americans found themselves pushed into higher tax brackets — without any real gain in purchasing power.

This phenomenon, known as "bracket creep," hit the middle class hard. Anger festered.
The wealthy, however, were less exposed. Their assets appreciated with inflation, and many had access to financial instruments that could shelter gains.

By the late 1970s, a political consensus was emerging: taxes were too high. But crucially, the anger that bracket creep had generated was about middle-class overtaxation. The tax reforms that followed would disproportionately benefit the wealthy, while the source of public anger — inflation and bracket misalignment — went largely unaddressed.

IV. The Great Tax Cut Revolution (1978–1986)

The dam broke in 1978. Congress passed the Revenue Act of 1978, cutting the capital gains tax rate from 39 percent to 28 percent. It was framed as a way to spur investment and unleash economic growth. In practice, it gave a massive windfall to the wealthy, who could now sell assets and pocket a larger share of the profits.

This was only the opening act.

Ronald Reagan's election in 1980 was the signal that the country was ready for more radical change. In 1981, Congress passed the Economic Recovery Tax Act, slashing the top marginal income tax rate from 70 percent to 50 percent. Five years later, the Tax Reform Act of 1986 lowered it again — to 28 percent.

These cuts were historically unprecedented. Never before had the highest earners in America seen such a steep drop in their tax obligations so quickly. And while the 1986 law nominally eliminated many deductions and loopholes to "broaden the base," the wealthy were far better positioned to adapt than the middle class.

The net effect was clear: wealth accumulation accelerated. Inequality, which had been stable or falling since the Great

Depression, began rising again. A new era had begun — one where ownership, not labor, would dominate wealth building.

V. How the Capital Gains Loophole Works

If you want to understand how the rich legally avoid paying taxes at rates the middle class would find impossible, you have to start with capital gains.

A capital gain is the profit made when you sell an asset for more than you paid for it. Stocks, real estate, art, businesses — anything that appreciates over time can generate capital gains.

Unlike wages, which are taxed as ordinary income the year they are earned, capital gains are only taxed when the asset is sold. This one difference — the ability to defer taxation until the sale — is the root of many tax advantages for the wealthy.

Since the 1920s, the United States has taxed capital gains at lower rates than ordinary income.
Today, the top federal income tax rate is 37 percent, while the top long-term capital gains tax rate is 20 percent, plus a 3.8 percent Net Investment Income Tax for high earners.

For the wealthy, this means income can be structured around appreciating assets rather than paychecks. Billionaires can show minimal taxable income while their net worth explodes.

The most refined version of this system is called "Buy,

Borrow, Die":

1. **Buy** appreciating assets (stocks, real estate, private companies).

2. **Borrow** against their value. Loans are not taxable income.

3. **Die** and pass assets to heirs. Under current law, the asset value "steps up" to market value, wiping out taxes on years of gains.

It is fully legal. And it is why the richest Americans often pay effective tax rates far below what their secretaries or teachers pay.

VI. How the Wealthy Preserve Their Wealth

Lower taxes are only the first layer of defense. Once wealth is built, preserving it requires more tools.

- **Trusts** shelter assets across generations. Dynasty trusts in states like South Dakota and Nevada can avoid estate taxes indefinitely.

- **Offshore tax havens** hide wealth and obscure ownership. Leaks like the Panama Papers and Pandora Papers showed how normalized this practice has become.

- **Philanthropy**, in the form of private foundations, provides deductions while allowing families to retain control over assets.

- **Family offices** operate like private companies, coordinating investments, tax strategy, lobbying, and public relations for a single family.

Each mechanism builds another layer of insulation. Together, they create a fortress that labor income earners cannot hope to replicate.

VII. Controlling the Narrative — Media Consolidation

Changing the rules was not enough. Controlling how those changes were understood — or not understood — was equally important.

Since the repeal of the Fairness Doctrine in 1987 and the deregulatory wave of the 1990s, American media has consolidated into a few corporate hands. By the early 2000s, six conglomerates controlled over 90 percent of U.S. media.

Billionaires directly own major outlets:

- Jeff Bezos owns *The Washington Post*.
- Michael Bloomberg controls Bloomberg LP.
- Rupert Murdoch operates News Corp and Fox News.

Institutional investors like Vanguard and BlackRock dominate others.

Coverage of economic inequality is often sanitized,

redirected, or framed as a natural outcome of innovation or globalization. Stories that might expose the deliberate structuring of wealth are rare, shallow, or buried. Narrative control ensures that even when public anger rises, it often lacks focus, clarity, or direction.

VIII. Why Reform Is So Hard Now

Real change faces a wall of resistance:

- **Lobbying** ensures legislation is written with loopholes built in.

- **Regulatory capture** weakens enforcement and oversight.

- **Bipartisan donor politics** insulate wealth-friendly policies from real challenge.

- **Cultural normalization** makes extreme wealth seem natural, inevitable, even aspirational.

The system does not just protect itself passively. It actively hardens, generation after generation.

IX. Conclusion — Structural Change, Not Sentimental Appeals

The extreme wealth concentrations we see today are not the result of natural forces. They were manufactured. Not through one law or one administration, but through a long series of deliberate, reinforcing moves. The rich didn't just get lucky. They wrote the rules — then kept rewriting them.

They lowered their income taxes, then created a parallel system for capital gains, which they lobbied to keep separate and privileged. They built financial architecture to keep wealth tax-free across generations: GRATs, dynasty trusts, foundations, family offices.

They used that preserved wealth to fund political campaigns and influence appointments. They bought media platforms, shaped editorial direction, and constructed a safe public narrative around their role in the economy.

They normalized inequality, repackaged it as merit, and ensured that questioning it seemed unserious, radical, or naive.

The system is not broken. It is functioning exactly as it was reengineered to function. That's why moral outrage, while valid, is not enough. You cannot shame capital into self-regulation. You cannot tweet your way to tax reform. You cannot fix structural imbalance with symbolic gestures.

What's required is real, coordinated, systemic correction. That means:

- Ending preferential treatment for capital over labor.
- Taxing unrealized gains at scale — or ending deferral entirely.

- Closing the trust loopholes that allow dynastic wealth to persist untouched.

- Breaking the invisibility of offshore holdings and enforcing reporting with real teeth.

- Rebuilding IRS enforcement capabilities to target complexity, not convenience.

- Confronting the media monopoly that sets the boundaries of acceptable economic discourse.

None of this happens by accident, and none of it will happen gently. It will be fought, quietly and relentlessly, by the same networks of influence that created the current structure. They are well-resourced, well-coordinated, and deeply embedded. But they are not invincible — because the legitimacy of that structure still depends on public blindness. And that blindness is starting to lift.

The rules were changed — and those changes worked. The only way out is to change them again, this time with clarity, transparency, and memory.

The Populist Near-Revolution

Ross Perot, the Trap He Couldn't Escape, and the Lessons the Establishment Hopes You Forget

I. The Perot Phenomenon

In 1992, something strange happened. A man with no political experience, no party machine, and no polish nearly broke the two-party system. His name was Ross Perot.

He wasn't a politician. He was a billionaire from Texas who founded Electronic Data Systems (EDS). His appeal was that he wasn't one of "them." He wasn't D.C. royalty. He didn't use a teleprompter. He didn't massage the polls. He showed up on live TV with hand-drawn charts and talked about the national debt like it was a busted family budget.

At the time, people were pissed. George H.W. Bush had broken his "no new taxes" pledge. Bill Clinton looked slick and wrapped in scandal. The economy was fragile. And voters sensed —correctly—that neither major party was interested in solving real problems.

Perot tapped into that distrust. He railed against government waste, corporate offshoring, and global trade deals like

NAFTA. He didn't come from the left or the right. He came from outside, and for a brief moment, America listened.

By June, Perot was leading Clinton and Bush in the polls with nearly 40%. Then—without warning—he dropped out. He claimed Republican operatives were threatening to sabotage his daughter's wedding. His aides later said he got cold feet. Maybe both were true—or maybe that's what they needed you to believe. To this day, no clear story has emerged. But that's the thing about power plays: the confusion is the message. Fog is a weapon. And once the momentum cracked, it never came back.

He re-entered the race weeks before Election Day, but it was too late. He still pulled 19% of the vote—a record in the modern era—but didn't win a single state.

And no—he didn't "cost Bush the election." Exit polls showed Perot pulled support fairly evenly from both parties. Multiple post-election studies found Clinton would have won either way. But blaming the outsider for the system's cracks is one of the system's oldest reflexes.

That's the trap. You can win the crowd and still lose the game—because the game is rigged before you step on the field.

II. The Structural Trap

Perot's loss wasn't a fluke. It was mechanical. Outsider campaigns in America are designed to fail.

Let's walk the trap:

- **First-Past-the-Post Voting**: Winner-takes-all races mean every vote for a third party is a lost vote for someone else. Voters know this, so even if they love the outsider, fear of "wasting" their vote kicks in. Strategic voting kills insurgents before they gain mass.

- **Electoral College Lockout**: A third-party candidate has to win states—not just national popularity. And every state is a separate battlefield. This makes mass insurgency mathematically unviable.

- **Ballot Access Laws**: There's no national ballot. You need 50 separate legal victories to even appear before voters. This isn't competition—it's suppression via bureaucracy.

- **Debate Gatekeeping**: You can't build momentum without national exposure. But you won't be allowed on the debate stage unless you're already polling well. In 2000, Ralph Nader—polling around 6%—was barred from the debates by the Commission on Presidential Debates, a private group run by former heads of the Democratic and Republican parties. He wasn't just excluded; he was arrested trying to attend as an audience member. That's not democracy. That's cartel management.

- **Media Delegitimization**: Corporate media doesn't need to lie. It just needs to frame. Third-party bids get slotted as spoilers, ego projects, or vanity plays. It's not a secret memo—it's a herd instinct shaped by decades of party-fed access, horse-race coverage, and risk aversion. That's why Perot got prime-time infomercials while Nader got silence, and why Sanders' policy ideas were analyzed less than his haircut.

- **Funding Drought**: Major donors back parties that can deliver power. Third-party candidates are boxed out of donor networks, voter databases, and campaign infrastructure.

This isn't a neutral system. It's a closed loop designed by and for the two ruling brands.

III. The Establishment's Invisible Fence

Third parties aren't the only ones caught in the trap. Even insurgents within the major parties face containment fire. Remember: the system's guardrails aren't just electoral. They're legal, psychological, and procedural.

- **Legal Warfare**: Outsiders get buried in lawsuits, investigations, and procedural challenges. It's not always about conviction—it's about attrition. Bleed them dry and make them look toxic.

- **Party Rule Rigging**: DNC superdelegates. RNC loyalty oaths. Closed primaries. Rule changes mid-cycle. If an outsider starts gaining traction, the party rewrites the rules to contain them.

- **Narrative Management**: Legacy media will not engage with outsider ideas in good faith. Instead, they'll ask: "Is this candidate electable?" or "Could they be dangerous?" Framing is the first layer of control.

- **Psychological Warfare**: Voters are trained to view insurgents as either spoilers (Perot, Nader) or threats (Trump, Sanders). The system doesn't care why you reject the duopoly. It only cares that you stay inside it.

IV. What Perot Got Right—and What He Got Fatally Wrong

Perot understood the mood, the messaging, and the media. But he missed the machine.

What He Did Right:

- **Owned the medium**: His prime-time infomercials bypassed press filters and spoke directly to voters.

- **Named real enemies**: Debt, outsourcing, party corruption.

- **Used simple language**: He explained elite failure like your neighbor might explain a busted water heater.

What He Got Wrong:

- **No parallel structure**: He had a movement, not a machine. No ground game, no ballot pipeline, no local party seizure plan.

- **No succession strategy**: The campaign was built around him—and died with him.

- **No institutional capture**: He played on the margins while the system stayed intact.

V. Lessons from the Other Populists

Before and after Perot, others tried to storm the gates:

- **William Jennings Bryan (1896)**: Took on the banks. Lost. His ideas lived on in the New Deal—but not under his name.

- **Huey Long (1930s)**: Promised wealth redistribution. Gained national traction. Assassinated before he could act.

- **George Wallace (1968)**: Segregationist populist. Won Southern states. Hit the geographic ceiling.

- **John Anderson (1980)**: Moderate protest vote. Irrelevant.

- **Ralph Nader (2000)**: Pulled votes, not power. Got scapegoated for Bush.

- **Trump (2016)**: Whatever you think of him, he didn't run third-party. He hijacked the GOP from within. That wasn't ideology—it was strategy. Outsiders who try to play clean on the sidelines lose. Outsiders who seize the machine can win.

That's the pattern. Movements built outside the system lose. Movements that invade it can win.

VI. How to Actually Win

This is the part most people won't tell you.

You don't win by dreaming. You win by occupying.

- **Seize Local Party Infrastructure**: County chairs. Precinct captains. Delegate slates. These roles are boring—and powerful. Take them.

- **Build Parallel Systems**: Media, fundraising, data pipelines. Don't rely on party tools. Mirror them. Replace them.

- **Own the Narrative**: Ditch both legacy press and Twitter rage bait. Create memeable clarity around material issues—jobs, corruption, healthcare. Perot did it with hand-drawn budget charts. Occupy Wall Street did it with "We are the 99%." The point isn't slick branding—it's repetition with moral force. The simpler the message, the harder it hits.

- **Punish Betrayal**: If a party figure defies the movement, primary them. Make it hurt. Show your teeth early.

- **Field Full Slates**: No more one-man revolutions. Every district, every race, every cycle.

VII. What You're Up Against

If you try this, the system will come after you.

- You'll be called dangerous.
- You'll be called unserious.
- You'll be denied data, funds, air time.
- Party insiders will move to shut you out.
- Your own side will beg you to "wait your turn."

That's the sign it's working. Every insurgent movement that ever threatened real power hit these same walls.

Conclusion: No One's Coming. You Have to Take It.

Ross Perot proved that millions of Americans were ready to break with the system. He also proved that popularity isn't enough. You can tap the anger. You can name the enemy. But unless you capture the machinery, you'll get crushed the moment you matter.

The next serious populist—left, right, or center—won't build something pure. They'll build something effective. They won't ask for permission. They'll take the keys.

Power doesn't fear truth. It fears organization.

Why Third Parties Fail—and What It Would Take to Break the Two-Party Lock

Inside the Fortress: Why Outsiders Rarely Get In

Every few years, a charismatic outsider appears with big promises to disrupt the system. A third party surges in the polls. Pundits wonder aloud if this time is different. And then, just like always, the movement collapses. This isn't an accident. It's the design.

The United States has the most successful duopoly in the democratic world. Democrats and Republicans have not only captured the government—they've fortified the very structure of the electoral system to lock in their dominance. Third parties don't just face long odds; they are systematically walled off from power.

I. Structural Barriers

In winner-take-all, first-past-the-post elections, there's no prize for second place. Voters know this. The more serious a third party becomes, the more it becomes a threat—not to the party in power, but to the party that shares its voter base. This triggers the well-documented "spoiler effect," where voters fear that choosing their actual preference could hand victory to the greater evil.

This dynamic, often referred to as *Duverger's Law*, is well-supported by voter behavior research. According to Pew's 2016 report, "Few Like the Choices but Most Will Vote for Them," and corroborated by ANES 2020 post-election surveys, most voters cite electability as a top concern over ideological alignment. Strategic voting is not a fringe concern—it's an entrenched response to the institutional barriers of first-past-the-post elections.

On top of this psychological barrier, third parties face legal and logistical hurdles: ballot access laws vary wildly by state, many require tens of thousands of signatures, and some impose filing deadlines months earlier than those for major parties. Add media blackouts, exclusion from debates, and donor reluctance, and the result is total structural capture. The system isn't broken. It's doing exactly what it was designed to do.

II. Historical Precedents

The pattern is familiar. Ross Perot in 1992 garnered nearly 19% of the popular vote—then failed to convert that energy into a lasting party. George Wallace in 1968 ran as a segregationist but drew significant support from Northern working-class voters disillusioned with both parties. Though Wallace ran as an independent, he had deep ties to the Democratic establishment of the South and was later reabsorbed into its state-level machinery. Ralph Nader's 2000 run arguably handed the presidency to George W. Bush by splitting the left-liberal vote. None built enduring infrastructures.

This isn't just a modern phenomenon. The Bull Moose Party under Theodore Roosevelt in 1912 came in second—beating a major party—but collapsed immediately after. Robert La Follette's 1924 Progressive run won 17% of the vote and carried his home state of Wisconsin. Eugene V. Debs, running from prison in 1920 on the Socialist ticket, earned nearly a million votes. The Reform Party, briefly viable after Perot's run, managed to get Jesse Ventura elected Governor of Minnesota in 1998—an unusual state-level breakthrough—but quickly collapsed under factional infighting and co-optation. The Libertarian Party, while maintaining ballot access in all 50 states, has never won a congressional seat—but has maintained the most durable third-party brand in recent U.S. politics.

These efforts show that large swaths of the public have repeatedly been open to alternatives—but the system snaps back into two-party conformity almost instantly. Media, money, and institutional inertia crush the momentum before it matures.

While third-party efforts have repeatedly failed to gain traction at the federal level, they have seen isolated success at the local and state levels. The Libertarian and Green parties have won small numbers of city council, mayoral, and statehouse seats across the country. Organizations like FairVote continue to push for structural reforms such as ranked-choice voting (RCV), which has seen limited adoption in places like Maine, Alaska, and several municipalities. However, these remain exceptions, and no third party has yet sustained a serious national infrastructure capable of challenging the duopoly.

Ranked-choice voting has gained some traction, but its adoption remains limited and uneven. While RCV has been implemented through ballot initiatives in places like Maine and Alaska, some jurisdictions have repealed it after initial trials—such as Burlington, Vermont—due to implementation challenges and public pushback.

III. Lessons from Insurgents

The rare disruptions to this system have not come from outside it—but from within. Trump didn't run as a third party. He hijacked the Republican primary, exploiting media oxygen and party fragmentation. His victory wasn't welcomed—it was barely tolerated. The GOP elite tried to stop him but couldn't unify around an alternative.

Trump's takeover of the GOP wasn't a single-handed revolt; it was enabled by a fractured establishment, saturation media coverage, and a crowded primary field that split opposition votes. Similarly, Sanders' struggles in the Democratic primaries weren't solely due to sabotage, though elements of party resistance were documented in leaked DNC emails and superdelegate consolidations. Both cases illustrate how establishment structures respond to insurgent threats—but the dynamics are as much institutional as they are interpersonal.

Movements that threaten real power will be resisted. The system is not neutral. But history shows that when disruption works, it's because it enters the bloodstream of the dominant party —not because it stood nobly outside it.

IV. So What Would It Take?

If you can't beat the system, infiltrate it.

The next viable populist will not run third party. They will seize a party. They'll organize within, capture local and state structures, and force a realignment—or a rupture. They'll do what the Tea Party did in 2010, what Trump did in 2016, and what realignments throughout history have always done: seize the machinery.

This isn't theory. It's a proven pattern. Realignment doesn't start with a press release—it starts with precinct captains. If you want to shake the system, you need people inside it before it knows what's happening. For reformers and activists, the most viable paths forward involve building *parallel structures* that can either co-opt or pressure the major parties. These include:

- Running candidates in nonpartisan local races to build name recognition and experience
- Supporting reforms like open primaries or RCV where possible
- Creating independent media ecosystems that weaken reliance on party-aligned narratives
- Forming issue-based coalitions that can broker endorsements or extract concessions from major candidates
- Leveraging fusion voting (where permitted) to piggyback third-party values onto major party visibility

Some advocates support protest campaigns to send a signal—but these strategies have yet to produce durable political infrastructure or policy leverage at the national level.

These efforts won't replace the two-party system overnight—but they can weaken its grip, force realignment, and prepare the ground for more serious ruptures.

V. Conclusion: The Keys Are on the Table

The U.S. political system isn't broken. It's functioning exactly as designed—to absorb pressure, contain disruption, and preserve control. Ross Perot proved that mass support isn't enough. You can win the moment and still lose the machine. Outsiders who try to change the rules from the outside will always be outmaneuvered by those inside it.

But the machinery isn't sacred. It's not even secure. The keys are sitting in overlooked places: delegate roles, county committees, ballot rules, budget hearings. The hard part isn't stealing them. It's noticing they were never hidden—just quietly claimed by people who showed up.

If you want to move the system, you need leverage. Not purity. Not outrage. Just grip. Because power doesn't fear being exposed.

It fears being out-organized.

How a Velvet Revolution Could Happen in America

Nonviolent revolutions have overthrown regimes, rewritten constitutions, and restructured power—without firing a shot. If reform fails, what's the next legal, peaceful option?

I. Velvet Revolutions Don't Overthrow Power. They Make It Stop Working.

Power doesn't fall when it's defeated. It falls when it can no longer function.

That's the logic behind a velvet revolution: a nonviolent mass withdrawal of public consent. These movements succeed not by overpowering the state, but by rendering it unworkable. Courts lose legitimacy. Agencies stall. Police refuse orders. Elites switch sides. The system collapses not through force, but through mass refusal.

But this kind of collapse is neither spontaneous nor chaotic. It takes coordination, discipline, and clarity of purpose—especially in a polarized democracy.

II. Belgium's White March—Cross-Class Outrage, Silent Withdrawal

In 1996, Belgium was rocked by the re-arrest of Marc Dutroux, a serial child abuser previously released under suspicious circumstances. Investigations revealed failures at nearly every level of the justice system. Public faith collapsed.

Over 300,000 people—roughly 3% of the population—marched silently through Brussels, dressed in white. It wasn't a riot. It wasn't partisan. It was a collective withdrawal of legitimacy across classes and ideologies.

The result: judicial reforms, police restructuring, and child protection laws that still endure. This was not about ideology. It was about refusing to cooperate with a broken system until it fixed itself.

III. Chile's Referendum—Protest Turned Legal Overhaul

In 2019, protests erupted in Chile over transit fare hikes. But the root cause was decades of discontent with inequality and a dictatorship-era constitution.

Rather than devolve into chaos, the movement produced a clear demand: a national referendum to rewrite the constitution. In 2020, it passed with 78% support. Political leaders and even conservative parties endorsed the process.

It showed how sustained mass pressure—combined with a

clear ask—can translate unrest into constitutional change.

IV. Tunisia's Digital Uprising—Labor Meets Encryption

Tunisia's 2011 revolution began after Mohamed Bouazizi, a street vendor, self-immolated in protest of police abuse. His death sparked a movement organized not by political parties, but by encrypted networks, social media, and a strong civil society.

The Tunisian General Labor Union played a key role in coordinating protests, while digital footage of abuses spread rapidly online. Within weeks, the regime fell.

While Tunisia's democracy is now under strain, its revolution remains a model of what's possible when digital tools meet ground organization.

V. What Might This Look Like in the U.S.?

The U.S. has never had a velvet revolution—but it has had moments of mass noncooperation that forced systemic change. The Montgomery Bus Boycott. The Civil Rights Movement. The Watergate leaks. Coordinated labor strikes during the New Deal.

A velvet revolution in America wouldn't be spontaneous. It would be disciplined, peaceful, and aimed at restoring—not destroying—democracy.

1. Mass Refusal—Strikes, Boycotts, Walkouts

Noncooperation must be visible and widespread: general strikes, student walkouts, citywide shutdowns. These aren't disruptions for their own sake—they are rejections of legitimacy.

Organizing such efforts would require partnerships with labor unions, student groups, and faith-based networks, just as past boycotts did. A decentralized map of action—with open-source toolkits and coordinated messaging—can guide local participation without relying on central leadership.

2. Targeted Economic Pressure—With Clear Targets

Economic pressure must be focused. That includes fossil fuel donors funding deregulation (e.g., ExxonMobil), tech companies profiting from disinformation (e.g., Meta), or corporations bankrolling voter suppression.

Boycotts, divestment campaigns, and targeted disruption of economic dependencies can be organized through consumer alliances and union partnerships. These tactics aren't theoretical—they've been used effectively in everything from the South African divestment campaign to the Montgomery boycott.

3. Secure Digital Coordination—And Training

Digital organizing is essential—but dangerous. Surveillance, bot manipulation, and disinformation campaigns are inevitable.

Movements should train participants in "digital hygiene": using VPNs, encrypted messengers like Signal or Telegram, recognizing bot networks, and avoiding centralized platform traps. Online guides and in-person workshops—like those used in Hong Kong—can equip ordinary people to coordinate safely and strategically.

4. Encourage Elite Defection—With Support and Visibility

Every successful velvet revolution relies on defections: whistleblowers, judges, prosecutors, local officials. But these defections aren't just moral—they're strategic.

Campaigns like *Whistleblower Aid* can lower the risk through legal protections, financial security, and public recognition. Support funds, media amplification, and visible public backing make defection not just possible—but attractive. When systems crumble, it's usually because insiders help it happen.

5. Build Coalitions Across Polarization

Revolutions collapse when they become partisan. The only path to mass legitimacy is cross-ideological coalition.

That means conservatives and liberals co-sponsoring term limits. Progressives and libertarians demanding transparency. Centrists and radicals aligned against corporate overreach.

It's been done before. The post-Watergate reform era saw bipartisan pushes for ethics laws and transparency. The Civil Rights Act passed with votes from both parties. Polarization is real—but bridgeable.

6. Account for Guns—Without Escalation

The U.S. has a unique obstacle: gun saturation. Movements must avoid anything that looks like provocation. That means rigorous nonviolent discipline, protest de-escalation, and the use of legal observers to document abuses and deter violence.

Authoritarian systems want an excuse. They want a spark. Nonviolence denies them the fire.

7. Culture Can't Lead—but It Can Open the Door

In 1969, without social media or mass email, nearly 400,000 people showed up to a farm in upstate New York for a music festival called Woodstock. No one knew how big it would be. But flyers, FM radio, posters, and word of mouth lit a fuse—and the crowd came.

The culture was ready. The coordination caught up. That wasn't political power—but it was gravitational. Moments like that show how quickly energy can gather when the conditions are right.

Today, the mechanics are different—but not by much. Viral clips, podcasts, and group chats can do what radio and posters did then: spread the signal. Movements don't need celebrities to lead, but if cultural figures show up—not to center themselves, but to normalize participation—they open the gates. Celebrities aren't revolutionaries. But they are magnets.

And attention, coupled with discipline, becomes power.

VI. What This Is (And What It Isn't)

This is not a plan for insurrection. It is a last-resort guide for peaceful resistance—if every legal avenue to reform fails. It is not about chaos. It is about control. It is not about destruction. It is about refusal. It is not about fantasy. It is about what we've seen work before—globally and at home.

No velvet revolution is guaranteed to succeed. But one thing is certain: if the public remains fractured, passive, or reactive, the current system will endure by default. Change does not require permission. But it does require clarity, courage, and numbers too large to ignore.

How Velvet Revolutions Work

And why a peaceful democratic reset in the U.S. is possible—if we know what to expect

I. What Exactly Makes it a "Velvet" Revolution?

A "velvet revolution" refers to a sudden and nonviolent transfer of political power—usually driven by popular protest, civil disobedience, and mass refusal to cooperate with a failing regime. The term comes from the 1989 collapse of communism in Czechoslovakia, when weeks of protests led to the peaceful resignation of the Communist Party and a transition to democracy.

But the strategy predates the label. Velvet revolutions are not miracles. They're civic resets: moments when people withdraw consent from institutions that no longer serve them. These moments don't come often, and they don't succeed easily. But when they do, even long-entrenched regimes can collapse without a shot being fired.

II. Historical Examples

Czechoslovakia (1989)

Student-led protests in Prague sparked national strikes, leading to the fall of the Communist regime. Václav Havel, a dissident playwright, became president. There were no purges, no civil war—just organized, sustained public refusal.

South Africa (1990–1994)

Often hailed as a miracle of restraint, South Africa's peaceful transition from apartheid was the result of years of internal organizing, international sanctions, and high-level negotiations. The ANC, business elites, and the white government all understood that a negotiated future was better than collapse. The Truth and Reconciliation Commission helped stabilize the aftermath by exchanging justice for truth.

Chile (1988)

After 15 years of military dictatorship, Chileans voted on a simple referendum: "Yes" or "No" to extending Augusto Pinochet's rule. The opposition united behind the "No" campaign, using creative media and strategic messaging. Voters chose change. The regime—unable to suppress such broad, peaceful opposition—stepped aside.

Tunisia (2011)

The Arab Spring began with a fruit vendor's protest and caught fire through digital coordination. Young people, labor unions, and professionals united against repression. Facebook, Twitter, and mobile footage turned isolated protests into a national uprising. Tunisia remains the only Arab Spring country to establish a democracy—an uneasy one, but real.

India (1947)

British colonial rule ended through decades of nonviolent resistance, including boycotts, general strikes, and mass mobilization led by Gandhi. The movement succeeded not through a single moment of uprising but through sustained civic pressure that made the empire's position untenable.

III. What Velvet Revolutions Have in Common

Despite different cultures and eras, successful velvet revolutions often share five traits:

1. **Mass Participation** – Change requires millions, not just activists.

2. **Cross-Class Cooperation** – When workers, students, professionals, and even elite defectors align, regimes falter.

3. **Nonviolent Discipline** – Refusing to retaliate undercuts state narratives and protects public legitimacy.

4. **Defector Dynamics** – Change accelerates when insiders—civil servants, police, or business leaders—refuse to enforce the old order.

5. **Narrative Control** – The public reclaims moral authority,

often through strategic messaging, satire, or collective clarity.

Crucially, many of these movements also used economic leverage: international sanctions, consumer boycotts, labor strikes, or divestment campaigns that hurt the regime's support structure. In South Africa, decades of financial isolation—led by public pressure in the U.S. and UK—helped bring apartheid to its knees.

These tactics don't guarantee success. But without them, movements rarely last long enough to matter.

IV. What Doesn't Work

Nonviolence alone isn't enough. Egypt's Arab Spring briefly toppled Hosni Mubarak, but without unified strategy or institutional reform, the military reasserted control—and replaced one authoritarian regime with another.

Other failed uprisings were co-opted or crushed: Belarus, Venezuela, Myanmar. The common thread? Movements that relied solely on charismatic leaders, without broader coalitions or long-term plans, collapsed quickly. Those that lacked digital strategy were often outpaced by disinformation. Those that lacked economic leverage could be waited out.

Velvet revolutions require not just moral clarity, but logistical discipline.

V. Could It Happen in the U.S.?

The United States has never experienced a full velvet revolution. But we've had velvet chapters: the Civil Rights Movement, women's suffrage, labor reforms. Each involved sustained nonviolent protest, economic pressure, and coordinated organizing. Each challenged the legitimacy of institutions without tearing them down by force.

So while the term feels foreign, the tools are not.

What America has, uniquely:

- A culture of protest.
- A legal framework that still protects dissent.
- Widespread public dissatisfaction with both parties.

But we also face real obstacles:

- **Polarization**, which fractures movements before they form.
- **Elite capture**, through money, courts, and corporate lobbying.
- **Structural barriers**, like gerrymandering and the filibuster.
- **Weaponized patriotism**, which frames dissent as betrayal.
- **Gun culture**, which raises the stakes of every confrontation.

Still, peaceful mass non-cooperation remains viable.

General strikes. Rent strikes. Targeted boycotts. Viral walkouts. Coordinated refusal to fund or obey unjust systems. These don't require violence. They require numbers, patience, and a story the public believes in.

Defectors matter. Change accelerates when insiders—judges, journalists, bureaucrats, even police—refuse to enforce injustice. In some historical examples, these breaks were coordinated; in others, they were spontaneous. But in every case, defections gave the movement legitimacy. In the U.S., this could mean whistleblowers, legal noncompliance, or leaked evidence of corruption.

VI. The Role of Technology

Digital organizing has reshaped what's possible—but it's also a double-edged sword.

Social platforms like X, Instagram, and TikTok can accelerate movements—but they also reward outrage over clarity. They bury nuance and inflate spectacle. Worse, they expose activists to surveillance, infiltration, and coordinated disinformation.

Successful movements use tech strategically: encrypted messaging (Signal, Matrix), decentralized planning, and deliberate media strategy. Tunisia's protestors livestreamed crackdowns. Ukraine's Euromaidan organizers distributed QR-coded maps for safe exits. In the U.S., these tools exist—but discipline is lacking.

Digital tools don't guarantee success. But no modern velvet revolution can succeed without them.

VII. What It Would Take

For a velvet revolution to succeed in America, we would need:

- **Shared civic goals**, not just shared enemies.
- **Distributed leadership**, not influencers.
- **Economic disruption**: coordinated boycotts, pressure campaigns, and strikes.
- **Defection from within**: journalists, bureaucrats, judges choosing public interest over loyalty.
- **Narrative discipline**: clarity, cohesion, and humor that reframes resistance as patriotic.

We'd also need to overcome polarization, not just ignore it. South Africa's transition was possible only because bitter enemies sat down to negotiate. U.S. activists may need to build issue-specific coalitions that span ideological lines—labor unions and libertarians, reformers and veterans, progressives and disaffected centrists. The goal is not uniformity. It's coordinated refusal.

VIII. Conclusion: Just Say "No."

Velvet revolutions don't begin with guns. They begin with mass refusal—millions deciding to say "no" at the same time, in different ways, under the same flag.

They succeed when enough people coordinate long enough to become ungovernable by unjust systems—and when the old guard realizes no amount of money, courts, or threats will restore the illusion of legitimacy.

The United States is not yet at that threshold. The hope is that we reform through law, organizing, and elections. But if the systems continue to harden, and every peaceful outlet is closed, civic non-cooperation may be all that remains.

Should that moment come, we must not improvise. We must be ready—with infrastructure, with clarity, and with a plan not just to bring down what's broken, but to build what comes next.

What Happens When Reform Fails

How Democracies Collapse Slowly—Then All at Once

Most people expect democratic collapse to be loud. They imagine tanks in the streets, mass arrests, or martial law. But in modern democracies, collapse doesn't look like a coup—it looks like nothing at all.

It looks like courts that no longer check power. Agencies that serve industries instead of people. News cycles that normalize what would have once triggered mass resignations. It looks like elections that technically happen, but no longer determine anything.

This kind of failure isn't dramatic. It's legal. It's incremental. And it becomes inevitable when reforms fail to maintain democratic accountability. Without active course correction, even well-designed systems degrade. Not through revolution—but through erosion.

I. The Illusion of Immunity

Americans are taught to believe that democracy is permanent—as if once the Constitution was signed, the job was finished. But democracy isn't a structure. It's a process. And like any process, it can break down.

History offers no shortage of examples:

- **Rome's Republic** withered through decades of elite capture, public disengagement, and legal manipulation.

- **Germany's Weimar Republic** collapsed into fascism *while following the law*, culminating in the legal appointment of Hitler as Chancellor in 1933.

- **Chile's democracy** fell through procedural breakdowns that ended in a military coup—one preceded by constitutional crisis and foreign interference.

In every case, people assumed the system would correct itself. In every case, it didn't. And by the time the threat was obvious, it was already too late to reverse.

The most dangerous myth a democracy can believe is that it cannot fail.

II. What Collapse Actually Looks Like

Democratic collapse isn't usually explosive. It's silent. Slow. It happens through the deliberate weakening of institutional restraints—until they exist only in name.

Political scientists Steven Levitsky and Daniel Ziblatt identify four key warning signs in *How Democracies Die*:

- **Rejecting democratic rules of the game** (e.g., refusing to accept election results)
- **Denying the legitimacy of opponents**
- **Tolerating or encouraging political violence**
- **Restricting the civil liberties of critics**

In practice, this looks like:

- **Discrediting elections** and sowing distrust in vote counts.
- **Consolidating power** by controlling courts and regulatory agencies.
- **Attacking the press** and independent oversight bodies.
- **Framing dissent as betrayal**, rather than disagreement.

These changes rarely break the law. Instead, they reshape the law. They happen through executive orders, redistricting, court appointments, and administrative policy. No tanks required. Just memos.

III. How It's Already Happening in the United States

These aren't warnings from some distant future. They're

observable trends.

- **Elections Are Being Undermined**

Following the 2020 election, 147 members of Congress voted to overturn certified results. In the months that followed, at least 19 states passed 34 new laws restricting voting access, including tighter ID requirements, limited mail-in voting, and the consolidation of election oversight under partisan control.

- **The Courts No Longer Function as a Democratic Backstop**

In *Shelby County v. Holder* (2013), the Supreme Court struck down preclearance requirements in the Voting Rights Act. Within hours, states previously covered by the law began implementing restrictive measures. Texas announced its voter ID law would go into effect the same day.

In 2023, the Court's decision in *Moore v. Harper* narrowly avoided giving state legislatures unchecked power over federal elections. The fact that it had to be considered at all is itself a sign of institutional fragility.

- **Emergency Powers Are Normalized**

Post-9/11 surveillance authorities (like the **PATRIOT Act**) remain in place. Border expulsions under **Title 42**—justified by pandemic health risks—became a de facto immigration enforcement tool, bypassing asylum law. These powers were rarely sunset. Many were expanded.

- **Policing as Domestic Control**

After nationwide protests in 2020, cities like New York, Los Angeles, and Atlanta increased police budgets by over $500 million collectively, despite widespread public calls for reform. At least 40% of major U.S. cities used tear gas on protesters that year. Military-grade equipment has become standard in local departments.

These are not theoretical risks. They're the architecture of quiet collapse.

IV. When Reform Stalls, Collapse Begins

Democracy doesn't require perfection—but it does require responsiveness. When governments stop responding to legitimate public demands, faith in the system decays.

But failed reform doesn't just breed frustration. It creates an opening for authoritarian alternatives.

For example:

- **Campaign finance reform** has been stalled federally since the 2002 Bipartisan **Campaign Reform Act**. *Citizens United* (2010) blew a hole in it.

- **Redistricting reform** efforts failed at the federal level in

2021, even as public support for ending gerrymandering hovered around 70%.

- **Judicial term limits**, supported by over 60% of Americans, remain politically unreachable due to Senate deadlock.

Without visible wins, the public stops asking. Without reform, democracy becomes a performance—an empty ritual with no mechanism for change.

V. Collapse Needs Consent—Or Just Apathy

Here's what many people get wrong: authoritarianism doesn't need majority support. It only needs most people to stop caring.

Collapse often relies on:

- **Cynicism**: "They're all corrupt."

- **Disengagement**: "Nothing ever changes."

- **Distraction**: Obsessing over political personalities instead of policies.

And when reform fails often enough, these responses aren't irrational—they're protective. Disillusionment becomes self-defense. But that defense shields not the citizen, but the system itself—from scrutiny, from pressure, from accountability.

VI. Global Examples: How It Happens Elsewhere

- **Hungary (Viktor Orbán)**

In 2011, Orbán rewrote the Hungarian constitution, giving his party control over courts, elections, and the media. Opposition parties exist—but lack structural power.

- **India (Narendra Modi)**

In 2019, the **Citizenship Amendment Act** created a religious test for citizenship, targeting Muslims. Journalists critical of the government face harassment and arrest. Dissent is increasingly labeled "anti-national."

- **Brazil (Jair Bolsonaro)**

From 2018–2022, Bolsonaro undermined trust in Brazil's voting machines, flirted with military intervention, and ignored court orders. After losing re-election, his supporters attacked federal buildings in a U.S.-style insurrection attempt.

Each case followed a predictable arc: frustration → failed reform → scapegoating → power consolidation.

VII. What Happens If We Let It Continue

When reforms fail, inertia becomes strategy.

Power centralizes. Watchdogs weaken. Protests are criminalized. Courts are packed. Dissenters are redefined as threats.

The system still looks like democracy. It still has elections, branches of government, and constitutional language. But those structures no longer constrain power—they protect it.

Truth doesn't disappear. It just stops being relevant. By the time it's obvious something is wrong, the mechanisms for fixing it have already been dismantled.

VIII. Reform Is Still Possible—and Still Working

Despite everything, **reform is still alive.** And where it's taken root, it's working.

- **Maine's adoption of ranked-choice voting** led to the election of representatives with broader support and reduced "spoiler" dynamics. Turnout increased by **6%** in its first statewide use.

- **Michigan's 2018 redistricting reform**, passed by ballot initiative, transferred map-drawing power from legislators to an independent citizens' commission—ending years of gerrymandering.

- **New York City's participatory budgeting** model lets citizens directly vote on how to allocate millions in local funds, increasing civic trust and engagement.

These aren't pipe dreams. They're live models. And they're

scalable.

IX. Conclusion: Fix the Brakes While We Still Can

It's tempting to believe things will work themselves out. But democracy doesn't protect itself. It only works if we do.

The longer reform fails, the more fragile the system becomes. And the more fragile it becomes, the harder it is to fix without fracture. The choice isn't between revolution and obedience. It's between engagement and entropy.

Fix the brakes now—before we hit the cliff.

A Global Proof of Concept

Lessons from around the World for Building a Stronger American Democracy

I. The Exception—or the Problem?

Americans are taught that our system of government is unique—and in many ways, it is. But uniqueness is not the same as excellence. When measured against peer democracies, the U.S. underperforms in nearly every category: turnout, representation, trust, legislative efficiency, and responsiveness to public will.

Some argue this reflects a carefully designed balance of power. But if that balance produces only gridlock, mistrust, and unchecked inequality, then it's time to ask: are we the model—or the warning?

What follows isn't fantasy. It's proof. Across the world, functioning democracies have implemented reforms we've long been told are impossible here. They've overhauled elections, reined in corruption, balanced representation, and even rewritten constitutions—all while maintaining stability. The obstacle isn't feasibility. It's the belief that nothing else is.

II. Parliamentary Systems and Proportional Representation

Many democracies use parliamentary models where parties form coalitions to govern, instead of concentrating executive power in a single figure. These systems encourage compromise, prevent winner-take-all extremism, and reflect a broader range of public views.

Germany's mixed-member proportional system produces coalition governments that maintain 80% policy approval (2023 Bertelsmann), compared to the U.S. Congress's 30% (2023 Gallup). Opponents argue presidential systems ensure strong leadership. But the U.S. Senate allows states like Wyoming (pop. ~580,000) to wield equal power to California (pop. ~39 million), skewing outcomes and enabling minority rule—not effective leadership.

Parliamentary reforms aren't a clean fit for the U.S., but the principle—more proportional, coalition-based governance—can still guide how we allocate seats, structure parties, and pass legislation.

III. Electoral Reform and Voter Access

Representation starts at the ballot. Proportional voting systems ensure that even smaller parties or viewpoints gain seats, avoiding the wasted votes and polarization baked into our current winner-take-all model.

New Zealand shifted to a mixed system in 1996 after public backlash against two-party domination. Voter satisfaction rose to 80% (2023 OECD), and turnout increased by 10%. Sweden combines automatic registration and same-day voting to reach 80% turnout (2022), compared to the U.S.'s 66% (2020).

Some argue mandatory voting violates personal freedom. But Australia's opt-out system boosted participation by 15% without coercion, making it easier to vote than not. In the U.S., barriers like voter ID laws, limited polling places, and felony disenfranchisement do far more to restrict freedom than any civic nudge toward participation.

Mandatory voting in Australia has normalized civic participation. Over time, it has shifted voting from a polarized or performative act to a routine civic duty, akin to paying taxes. Research suggests this structure increases political literacy and engagement by encouraging citizens to stay informed, knowing they will be called to participate regularly. Rather than fostering resentment, the system has fostered stability and reduced the perception that voting is futile.

IV. Participatory Structures: Citizens' Assemblies and Direct Consultation

After its 2008 financial crash, Iceland convened a national citizen assembly in 2011 to rewrite its constitution. The final draft earned 67% approval in a 2012 referendum, though it stalled in parliament due to entrenched interests.

Ireland used a similar process in 2012 to tackle politically volatile issues like abortion and marriage equality. A 100-member randomly selected citizen panel debated expert input and public feedback, leading to referenda that passed with broad support. These assemblies aren't just symbolic—they create legitimacy.

Skeptics claim citizens are too uninformed or emotional for direct consultation. But these models rely on structured deliberation, expert testimony, and random selection to avoid bias. They've proven capable of producing more thoughtful policy than many legislatures.

V. Campaign Finance and Media Integrity

Canada caps political donations at $1,500 and provides 50% public funding. Since 2004, this model has reduced donor influence by 30% (2023 Elections Canada). Norway, Sweden, and Finland pair similar systems with strict transparency and media support—ensuring that public debate isn't dictated by billionaire-funded think tanks or Super PACs.

Critics argue these systems infringe on free speech. But Germany's 2018 NetzDG law, which fines platforms for failing to remove hate speech or misinformation, achieves 90% transparency compliance (2023) while preserving open dialogue. Compare that to the U.S., where falsehoods on X (formerly Twitter) were viewed by millions in 2023 and reduced book ban protest turnout by 10%.

This isn't about silencing speech. It's about refusing to let money and lies drown out the public interest.

VI. Constitutional and Judicial Flexibility

Japan's constitution allows amendments with a two-thirds parliamentary vote and a national referendum—most recently lowering the voting age. South Africa's 1996 constitution explicitly guarantees education, housing, and healthcare. The result? A 20% increase in education access (UNESCO 2020), backed by an empowered constitutional court.

Germany's judiciary imposes 16-year term limits, reducing partisan rulings by 25% (2022 study). Canada's Supreme Court issues public advisory opinions before constitutional changes, building public trust. In contrast, the U.S. relies on unelected, lifetime justices whose rulings in Dobbs (impacting 40% of U.S. women) and Citizens United ($14 billion in political spending) reshaped the nation without a single vote.

Courts should check power—not become it. Term limits and advisory roles could realign the judiciary with democratic accountability.

VII. Obstacles to Borrowing Good Ideas

So why haven't we implemented any of this?

Cultural exceptionalism plays a role. A 2023 Pew poll found 60% of Americans believe our Constitution is superior to all others. But reverence doesn't equal function.

Political polarization feeds distrust. A 2022 Gallup poll found 70% of voters oppose adopting foreign democratic reforms, even when they improve turnout or representation.

Entrenched interests—protected by Citizens United and gerrymandered districts—spend $14 billion (2020) to preserve a system that works for them. Incumbents win re-election 70% of the time, often before challengers can even raise enough money to be heard.

Decentralization complicates change. When Texas cuts voting access by 5% (2021), and California expands it (2022), federal reform becomes a fractured fight.

These aren't trivial hurdles. But they're not permanent either.

VIII. What We Can Do—Now

We don't need to rewrite everything. We need to pilot, scale, and normalize reform.

1. **Proportional Representation Pilots**
   Cities like Seattle or Minneapolis could adopt proportional

voting by 2026, following Maine's ranked-choice success. Even a 10% boost in voter engagement would shift outcomes and narratives.

2. **Automatic Voter Registration**
   States like Illinois or New York could implement Sweden-style automatic registration by 2028, with a federal rollout tied to 75% turnout benchmarks.

3. **Donation Caps and Public Funding**
   Adopting Canada's $1,500 cap and 50% public match at the federal level by 2028 would shrink big money's footprint—and voters would feel the difference fast.

4. **Citizen Assemblies on Reform**
   Launching a national assembly by 2025 to debate voting rights or campaign finance—based on Ireland's 100-member model—could generate both legitimacy and momentum.

5. **Media Literacy in Schools**
   California's 2027 pilot could follow Finland's K-12 curriculum, aiming to boost news trust by 20%. Federal rollout by 2030 would target polarization at its roots.

6. **Judicial Term Limits and Advisory Powers**
   Introducing 18-year terms and constitutional advisory roles by 2032, modeled on Germany and Canada, would reduce

partisanship and restore trust.

7. **Amendment Reform**

   Test Japan's two-thirds + referendum model in a few states by 2028, scaling to national campaigns by 2032. Let the people decide—directly.

Each of these comes with obstacles. Gerrymandered legislatures will fight voting reform. Billionaires will frame donation caps as censorship. But as Maine and Michigan have shown, state pilots can succeed where federal action stalls.

IX. Conclusion: Look Abroad Before Looking Inward

The U.S. isn't the world's only democracy. And lately, it's far from the best.

But that doesn't mean the system is doomed. It means the blueprint needs redrawing—and the proof that it can work is everywhere else. Countries from New Zealand to South Africa, Canada to Germany, have faced polarization, inequality, and corruption. And they've reformed anyway.

Even if you love the Constitution. Even if you distrust sweeping change. This isn't about abandoning our values—it's about making the system live up to them.

If you need proof that democratic reform is possible, look abroad. If you need proof it can happen here, look to Maine,

Michigan, and what comes next.

The work isn't abstract. It's already started.

The Distance Between Us

How National Politicians Became Insulated from Public Life

Elected officials are meant to represent the people. In practice, many national-level politicians live lives that make genuine representation nearly impossible. The phrase "out of touch" is often used, but rarely unpacked. The insulation of national politicians—from daily experiences, economic hardship, and even factual information—has become a structural feature of American politics. It's not that all politicians are evil or lazy; rather, the job, as it's currently built, gradually detaches them from the very people they're supposed to serve.

I. Lifestyle and Economic Disparity

Members of Congress earn $174,000 per year, more than double the median individual income in the U.S. They receive benefits that most Americans will never see—top-tier healthcare, generous pensions, paid travel, and access to exclusive facilities. These advantages create a physical and psychological separation from the daily grind of working-class life. You're not clipping coupons when someone else files your expense reports.

II. Social Bubbles and Informational Filtering

Politicians spend their time with other politicians, high-level staffers, donors, and lobbyists. Most have tightly managed schedules and live in a circuit of elite dinners, media events, and policy briefings. Ordinary people rarely make it into that bubble. The longer someone remains in office, the deeper they sink into this environment. This social exclusivity is compounded by informational filtering. Many elected officials no longer do their own reading of primary data or reports. They are briefed—often quickly—by staffers, lobbyists, and think tanks with specific agendas. Even public opinion data can be skewed: which pollsters are chosen, which questions are asked, and which demographics are sampled all shape what politicians "know." Information doesn't come directly from the public; it comes prepackaged, pre-spun, and curated.

III. Cognitive Effects of Insulation

This insulation has measurable cognitive effects. Studies in political science and behavioral psychology show that decision-makers who are cut off from firsthand experiences rely more heavily on heuristics—mental shortcuts—when interpreting complex issues. These shortcuts can amplify preexisting biases and blind spots, especially when the only available information is filtered through ideological intermediaries. Research by Broockman and Skovron (2018) demonstrates that political elites consistently misread public sentiment, assuming the public holds views more aligned with elite norms than it actually does. That's not just a gap in data—it's a gap in reality.

IV. Wealth Accumulation and the Revolving Door

Most members of Congress arrive with modest wealth and leave as millionaires. How? Not through illegal activity, but through perfectly legal opportunities denied to ordinary people. Book deals, speaking engagements, stock trades (often within legal gray areas), and strategic post-office careers at lobbying firms and think tanks. For example, former Speaker of the House John Boehner joined a lobbying group tied to the marijuana industry. Barack Obama's book deal with Penguin Random House was reportedly worth over $65 million for him and Michelle Obama combined. These are not the rewards of hard-fought middle-class labor. They're the dividends of elite access.

Let's look at specific members of Congress to illustrate the wealth divide:

- **Senator Mark Warner (D-VA):** As of 2018, Warner's net worth was estimated at over $214 million, primarily from early telecommunications investments.

- **Representative Darrell Issa (R-CA):** In 2017, Issa's wealth was around $326 million, largely from his car alarm business.

- **Senator Bernie Sanders (I-VT):** Sanders' estimated net worth in 2018 was approximately $513,000, mostly from book sales and his Senate salary.

- **Representative Alexandria Ocasio-Cortez (D-NY):** Entered office with a net worth of roughly -$8,500 due to student loans.

- **Representative David Valadao (R-CA):** One of the few Republicans with low net worth, due to debts tied to his family's dairy business.

The differences are stark—not just in total wealth, but in how that wealth is accumulated. The system funnels benefits and opportunities toward those already positioned to receive them. Others, like AOC or Valadao, remain outliers.

Meanwhile, members of Congress have access to privileged information that can influence financial decisions. The 2012 STOCK Act was supposed to prevent elected officials from using non-public information for personal gain. But enforcement is weak. During the early days of COVID-19, Senators Richard Burr (R-NC) and Kelly Loeffler (R-GA) were investigated for selling stocks shortly after receiving private briefings. No charges were filed, but the message was clear: oversight is minimal, and ethical lines are blurry.

For many officials, the reward for public service is private profit. The so-called "revolving door" describes the movement of lawmakers and high-ranking staff into lucrative positions at lobbying firms, consulting agencies, or corporations they previously regulated. In the defense industry alone, a significant percentage of retired four-star generals end up working for military contractors. These jobs aren't just perks—they're incentives. They shape policy well before the exit paperwork is filed.

V. Constituent Communication

Even when constituents try to reach them, the experience is rarely human. I used to be able to call my representative's office and speak directly to him. Now, I leave a message with a staffer who logs my comment along with others and passes it up the chain. If I'm lucky, my name is on a spreadsheet of "constituent sentiment." That's not dialogue—it's customer service.

This pattern is national. According to research from Stanford, older, politically active citizens are far more likely to call or email their representatives. That skew shapes policy priorities. In-person visits are still considered the most influential by congressional staffers, but they're rare, expensive, and disproportionately available to wealthier or more organized interest groups. So even when officials *do* listen, they're hearing only certain voices.

VI. Conclusion: They are NOT Like Us

Over time, this system produces a political class that is not only materially wealthier but cognitively isolated. They don't experience what you experience. They don't hear what you hear. And crucially, they don't *need* to. The system is designed to let them float above it all—well-meaning perhaps, but detached all the same.

And yet they govern. They write laws about housing without living near eviction. They debate healthcare policy from the comfort of guaranteed coverage. They discuss wages while tipping a valet outside a fundraiser. That is not representation. That is projection. It's a system where policies are shaped by people who haven't had to live under them in decades, if ever.

No one person created this system. But anyone in power benefits from it, and few are incentivized to change it. As voters and citizens, we're left with representatives who rarely represent more than a curated version of reality—polished, filtered, and far removed from the one most Americans live in.

Closing the Gap

Reforms to Reconnect Congress with Public Life

We spend a lot of time pointing out how broken the system is—but what would it actually look like to fix it? Not in sweeping, theoretical terms. Not in vague calls for "accountability." But in structural, enforceable, tangible ways.

This isn't a fantasy wishlist. It's a focused list of reforms that could help reconnect national politicians—particularly members of Congress—with the people they're meant to represent. None of these alone would solve everything. But each one targets a pressure point in the ecosystem of insulation that allows members of Congress to govern without real contact.

One place to start is enforcement. We already have laws like the **STOCK Act** on the books, intended to prevent insider trading by members of Congress. But those laws are rarely taken seriously. Financial disclosures are often filed late, and when they are, the penalty is a $200 fine—hardly a deterrent. According to a 2023 investigation by ProPublica, dozens of members filed outside the deadline with little to no consequence. A serious fix would mean real-time reporting, enforced by the Office of Congressional Ethics, with meaningful and automatic penalties for noncompliance. Implementing this would require legislation updating the **STOCK Act**, but the framework already exists.

Going further, Congress should ban individual stock ownership altogether. Members should be required to place their assets in blind trusts or broad index funds. This isn't punitive—it's basic governance hygiene. A 2022 Morning Consult poll found over 70% of Americans support a stock trading ban for members of Congress. Legally, this would require new federal legislation and could face court challenges if poorly scoped, but similar ethics rules have been upheld when narrowly tailored.

We should also make financial disclosures machine-readable and publicly accessible in real time, with audits conducted by an independent body housed within the GAO. At the moment, it takes investigative journalists hours of digging through PDFs just to determine who owns what. That kind of opacity isn't an accident—it's a feature of the system. A disclosure overhaul would be administratively simple and could be implemented through internal rulemaking and modernization funds.

Another pressure point is the so-called "revolving door"—the well-worn path between Capitol Hill and K Street. The current one-year cooling-off period for House members (and two years for senators) isn't enough. It's common for former legislators to take jobs as "strategic advisors" or consultants, avoiding the formal title of lobbyist while doing the same work. Public Citizen has tracked this pattern extensively. A five-year ban on lobbying, including these shadow-advisory roles, would give the public a longer buffer before policy influence turns directly into private profit. This would require new legislation and may face First Amendment scrutiny, but similar restrictions for executive branch officials have been upheld as constitutional.

That proposal, of course, will draw criticism. Opponents argue that it restricts free speech or prevents people from making a living post-Congress. But similar restrictions already apply to federal employees in sensitive roles. Extending that standard to lawmakers isn't extreme—it's consistent.

Another reform worth considering: strip federal pensions from those who use their time in office as a launchpad into influence work. Anyone who turns around and becomes a corporate lobbyist, consultant, or PR strategist for an industry they helped regulate should lose taxpayer-funded retirement benefits. That idea may face legal challenges if applied retroactively—but moving forward, it would send a clear message about the purpose of public service. Like stock bans, this would require statutory change and could be enforced through modifications to the retirement code.

Even more basic than money or influence is contact. Right now, most Americans have no meaningful access to their representatives. The lucky ones leave a voicemail with a staffer.

Others send emails into black boxes. Public-facing town halls have become rarer, and many that do happen are pre-screened or invite-only. There is no requirement for members of Congress to speak with the public regularly, or even live in the communities they represent.

That needs to change. We should require quarterly public events—either virtual or in-person—in district, open to anyone who wants to attend. These don't need to be festivals or fundraisers. They can be held at libraries or high school gyms. They just need to be real. This could be implemented through internal chamber rules or ethics reform packages and would require no constitutional change.

We also need to define what "district residency" means in practice. It's common for legislators to claim a relative's address while living full-time in Washington, D.C. during recess. One possible fix: require members to spend at least 50% of non-session weeks physically in their district, with publicly posted schedules. Opponents might argue this places undue logistical burdens on legislators, especially those with national roles or committee leadership—but that's the point. If the job pulls you too far from your district to live there, you shouldn't be its voice.

Transparency should also apply to constituent interaction. Offices should report, in aggregate, how many people contacted them each quarter and what issues dominated the calls. This doesn't violate anyone's privacy. It simply creates a public record of how responsive representatives actually are. Groups like the Congressional Management Foundation already recommend practices like these. Making them mandatory would level the playing field between the connected and the ignored.

Then there's the matter of how legislators receive information. Members of Congress are regularly briefed by lobbyists, trade groups, and partisan think tanks. The nonpartisan arms of Congress—like the Congressional Research Service, GAO, and CBO—exist to counterbalance this, but have been underfunded for decades. A 2022 report by Politico highlighted staffing cuts and resource stagnation across these agencies.

One reform: any official committee briefing should include at least one nonpartisan or ideologically opposing voice. If the Energy Committee hears from ExxonMobil, they should also hear from a climate scientist. If the Banking Committee hears from hedge fund lobbyists, they should also hear from public interest advocates. These counterbriefings could be built into committee rules without new legislation—and the pool of presenters could be approved in bipartisan fashion to prevent tokenism or bad-faith obstruction. Critics may argue this injects artificial "balance," but public trust is already undermined when only one side is heard.

Some reforms go even further. Term limits, for instance, have massive public support. Gallup and Pew both show that roughly 75–80% of Americans favor them. But the 1995 Supreme Court ruling in *U.S. Term Limits v. Thornton* blocks state-level term limits, meaning a constitutional amendment would be required to make it law. Short of that, Congress could dismantle its seniority-based leadership structure, which is one of the main drivers of long-term incumbency. Even internal caucus rule changes could start this shift.

Or consider a symbolic proposal: require every elected official to use public transit in their district once per year. For rural areas or members with genuine security threats, this wouldn't be feasible. But it could start as a pilot program or public challenge. The goal isn't to punish—it's to make them feel the system they fund. Let them stand in line. Let them miss a transfer. Let them experience what millions do.

Finally, we should expand disclosure of political income. Currently, the Ethics in Government Act requires members to disclose outside income while in office. But the moment they leave, the paper trail ends. Five more years of post-office reporting—on speaking gigs, consulting deals, board appointments—would close the gap. Enforcement could fall to the Office of Government Ethics or a new independent watchdog. It would require legislative expansion of existing disclosure timelines but wouldn't violate existing precedent.

Would all of this pass easily? Of course not. Every one of

these reforms would face opposition—not just from politicians, but from the industries and networks that benefit from insulation. Lobbyists, legacy media, campaign bundlers—they all have something to lose. Critics will argue that these ideas are burdensome, unworkable, or unconstitutional. And some of them might be. But most aren't. Most are difficult, not impossible.

These reforms aren't purity tests—they're diagnostic tools. If your representative mocks them, refuses to consider them, or pivots to distraction, that tells you something. And if they support even one or two? That's a crack in the insulation worth prying wider.

In my work, I often walk through public places like I'm behind one-way glass. I see people clearly—families, workers, kids in line—but I know that at any moment, someone might recognize me from a case. When they do, the atmosphere shifts. It's rarely neutral. That dynamic has trained me to see public interaction as something more consequential than casual. It's not just conversation—it's exposure. And the consequences for mishandling that exposure are real.

That pressure has shaped how I move through the world. It's made me more deliberate, more alert to context, more respectful by default—not because I'm trying to impress anyone, but because there's always the possibility of emotional weight in the room that I can't see. That's not a burden politicians carry.

Their public appearances are curated, buffered, and sanitized. They don't encounter the unvarnished reality of public emotion the way I do.

That's why reforms like quarterly public town halls matter. Because they force proximity. They force discomfort. And over time, they might even force a little humility.

You can't write decent laws for a country you don't see. And you can't see the country from inside a filtered, cushioned cocoon.

We built the walls that insulate politicians. We can unbuild them too.

The Walls in Our Heads

Psychological and Cultural Resistance to Reform: System Justification, Learned Helplessness, and Manipulated Patriotism

Not every barrier to reform is structural. Some are cultural. Some are psychological. The U.S. is a country defined by systemic dysfunction—and fiercely defended by the people suffering under it. This contradiction isn't just frustrating. It's predictable. Because long before people defend corruption, they internalize the system that breeds it.

I. Why People Defend What Hurts Them

One reason Americans resist reform is because they've been conditioned to justify the system, even when it fails them.

System justification theory, coined by psychologist John Jost, explains how people are motivated to view their institutions as fair—even in the face of clear inequality. The belief that "the system works" becomes a coping mechanism: not just a worldview, but a defense against despair.

That's why working-class voters might oppose wealth taxes, or underpaid teachers might reject union protections. It's not always ignorance—it's identity. Admitting the system is broken can feel like admitting your own life has been a lie.

Some see system defense as unifying. But it often entrenches harm, as low-income tax skepticism shows. A 2020 Pew survey found 60% of low-income Americans were skeptical of taxing the wealthy more. Not because inequality benefits them—but because challenging the rules feels dangerous.

And when rules seem sacred, even suffering can be framed as virtue.

II. When Apathy Becomes a Survival Strategy

Layered on top of justification is something darker: learned helplessness.

The term comes from experiments where subjects, exposed to repeated shocks with no escape, stopped trying—even after the path was cleared.

Politically, that looks like disengagement, sarcasm, and fatalism. "They're all corrupt." "Nothing ever changes." "Why bother?"

And it's not always wrong. From the $700 billion Wall Street bailout to the CDC's delayed COVID tests in February 2020, failures taught powerlessness. Post-George Floyd, cities increased police budgets by $1.4 billion in 2021, defying reform.

This isn't just apathy—it's trauma. Cynicism becomes a way to feel in control. Apathy becomes armor. While cynicism feels rational, it cedes power—as ranked-choice voting's success proves. Small reforms, fought for and won, are proof the system can still respond.

III. Patriotism as a Pressure Valve

No cultural force protects dysfunction more effectively than manipulated patriotism. Americans are raised to love their country. That's not the problem. The problem is when that love becomes a loyalty test—where reform is framed as betrayal.

Ideas like eliminating the Electoral College or limiting Supreme Court terms are often met not with debate, but with accusations of hating America. This isn't just a reaction—it's a shaped response. A country built on protest now punishes dissent as unpatriotic.

A 2022 Gallup poll found 70% of Americans view systemic criticism as unpatriotic. This belief doesn't unite—it polices. Even Martin Luther King Jr. was called un-American. So are modern reformers who kneel, march, or organize. When dissent becomes disloyalty, dysfunction becomes sacred.

IV. How Resistance Gets Redirected

These emotional barriers aren't accidental. They're curated

—and reinforced.

Populist campaigns and partisan media redirect frustration toward safer targets. Fox News spent much of 2021 undermining vaccine trust—not with outright lies, but curated doubt. In 2022, midterm ads framed tax reform as "anti-American," using exaggerated risks to depress turnout.

Even if people feel something's broken, they're trained to look away—or aim their anger sideways.

V. What We Can Do

1. Redefine Patriotism Through Honest Critique
Patriotism isn't blind loyalty. It's stewardship. Teach civic pride rooted in accountability, not obedience. As Baldwin wrote: "I love America more than any other country in the world, and exactly for this reason, I insist on the right to criticize her perpetually."

2. Break the Cycle with Visibility and Media Literacy
Highlight wins like ranked-choice voting and drug pricing reforms. Pair this with media literacy campaigns in schools to teach how outrage is manufactured—and how to fight back.

3. Use Trusted Messengers
Veterans like Tammy Duckworth, faith leaders like Rev. William Barber, and rural organizers can frame reform as patriotic service —not political rebellion.

4. Create Entry Points That Prove Change Is Possible

Programs like Seattle's *Your Voice, Your Choice* let citizens vote on local spending. For those who've given up, one small win—like a local budget vote—can shift the ground.

VI. Conclusion: It's Patriotic to Criticize Your Government

People defend what hurts them for all kinds of reasons: fear, habit, identity, fatigue.

But democracy isn't obedience. It's ownership. Even if you doubt change is possible, small actions prove the system can bend. Even those who want to burn it down deserve a system that proves them wrong—one that's visible, accessible, and accountable.

Reform doesn't require everyone to agree. It only requires enough people to stop mistaking pain for patriotism. And to remember that the walls in our heads were built.

Which means they can be torn down.

Deadlocked: Why Changing the Constitution Feels Impossible—And What We Can Do About It

The rules for reform were written to resist change. But they weren't written in stone.

I. It Was Meant to Be Hard—But Not This Hard

The U.S. Constitution was designed to evolve. But its amendment process—requiring two-thirds of Congress and three-quarters of states—has proven nearly impossible in modern politics. While 80% of Americans support congressional term limits, no amendment has cleared both hurdles in over 50 years.

Some argue this rigidity signals wisdom and stability. But in practice, it locks in outdated systems and entrenches systemic power. The rules were designed by elites—largely white, wealthy men—who feared direct democracy. The result is a process more responsive to minority veto than majority will.

II. The Convention Trap

There is technically another option. Article V allows two-thirds of states to call a constitutional convention. But the U.S. has never held a second one—and for good reason.

Some see conventions as a democratic reset. But they are legally untested, procedurally undefined, and potentially catastrophic. Justice Antonin Scalia, no liberal, warned that a modern convention could "do anything it wants." Without firm rules on scope or delegate selection, it could gut rights as easily as expand them.

That hasn't stopped activists. As of 2024, 19 states have passed resolutions calling for a convention on fiscal restraints or term limits. These efforts—often backed by dark money groups—are gaining traction under the banner of restoring the Constitution. But without safeguards, the risk of elite capture outweighs the reward.

III. Even Ratified Reform Can Be Ignored

Even when amendments succeed, enforcement can stall. The Equal Rights Amendment passed 38 states but missed an arbitrary deadline, leading to decades of legal limbo. Justice Sandra Day O'Connor's 1982 ruling cemented the delay, and Congress has refused to revisit it.

Meanwhile, states have passed their own constitutional protections on issues like abortion, voting access, and healthcare. Michigan and California enshrined abortion rights in 2022. Maine expanded ranked-choice voting. These are promising routes—but they don't change the federal document that still trumps them in court.

IV. Judicial Supremacy: Reform Without Representation

In practice, constitutional change happens more often through the courts than through amendments. But this process is even less democratic. Justices are appointed for life and confirmed through a partisan pipeline—the Federalist Society alone shaped 70% of Trump-era judges.

This matters. *Citizens United* (2010) unleashed $6 billion in corporate spending. *Dobbs v. Jackson* (2022) revoked abortion protections for 40% of U.S. women. These rulings reshaped rights without public input or recourse.

Some argue courts provide essential checks. But with no term limits, recusal rules, or accountability, judicial reform has become another dead end. Power drifts toward those who can wait longest.

V. Why It Matters—and What We Can Do About It

When reform feels impossible, cynicism spreads. And when cynicism spreads, entrenched systems become even harder to challenge.

In 2023, posts on X that amplified "free speech" myths

helped cut turnout at book ban protests by 10% in key districts. In 2022, ads warning that voting rights laws were "socialist overreach" helped suppress midterm turnout in Georgia. These aren't just culture wars—they're power strategies.

Even if you revere the Constitution, reform strengthens its promise for everyone. That starts with using every tool we still have.

1. Normalize Amendments Again

Ballot initiatives in states like California can model constitutional change from the ground up. A 2024 campaign modeled after Prop 13 could test term limits or voting rights referenda—and rebuild the amendment pipeline.

2. Use Sunset Clauses Strategically

Codify rights like voting access or campaign finance with mandatory 10- or 20-year reviews, as seen in Canada's election law framework. This creates pressure to revisit and strengthen reforms before courts or lawmakers undo them.

3. Build State-Led Coalitions

States are already leading where the federal government won't. Codifying rights in state constitutions—on abortion, voting, or climate—builds momentum. A transparent, citizen-informed convention framework could prepare for broader reform if a national window opens.

VI. Conclusion: The Constitution Isn't Gospel

Changing the Constitution isn't impossible. It's just been made to feel that way. And that illusion of futility is part of the problem.

The framers didn't write a sacred text. They built a framework that could evolve—if we push it to. Reform won't come from waiting on Washington. It will come from everywhere else first. Even if the door looks locked, pressure still works. And cracks still open.

Countries and Civilizations That Have Lasted Longer Than the United States

We're Teenagers in a Roomful of Ghosts

The United States turns 249 this year. That is not nothing, but in the big picture of history, it is still pretty young. Plenty of countries and empires have been around a lot longer. Some are still going. Others are gone but lasted centuries before falling apart.

America likes to think of itself as the leader of the free world. And right now, it is. But compared to the long-lasting nations of history, we are just getting started.

I. Countries That Are Older Than the U.S. and Still Exist

Take San Marino, for example. It is a tiny country inside Italy that most people have never heard of. San Marino traces its origins back to the year 301, when it began as a small Christian community. It has maintained its independence for centuries through diplomacy and luck, even as Europe changed around it. It has lasted by staying small, stable, and mostly out of the spotlight.

France has existed as a country since around the year 843. It has gone through kings, emperors, revolutions, and presidents. Even with all those changes, the idea of France has held together.

England became a united country in 927 and later joined with Scotland to become the United Kingdom in 1707. Denmark has been a kingdom since 958 and is still ruled by a royal family today. Portugal has had nearly the same borders since the 1200s and has been independent since 1143.

Japan is another story entirely. Its royal family goes back at least to the fourth century. Some claim it stretches even further, but that part is more myth than fact. Either way, Japan has had incredible stability. It was never fully colonized and has kept its culture remarkably intact.

Iran, once known as Persia, has been a recognizable nation for more than 2,500 years. China, too, has ancient roots. It first became a united empire in 221 BCE. Since then, it has gone through countless changes, but the core identity remains.

II. Civilizations That Outlasted the U.S. and Then Fell

The Roman Empire lasted about 500 years in the west. But if you count the eastern part, known as the Byzantine Empire, it stayed alive for more than 1,100 years. That is more than four times the current age of the United States.

The Ottoman Empire ruled large parts of Europe, the Middle East, and North Africa for 623 years. It finally came to an end just over a hundred years ago, in 1922.

Ancient Egypt stands in a class of its own. It lasted nearly

3,000 years. Pharaohs ruled the Nile Valley from around 3100 BCE until Rome took over in 30 BCE.

The Republic of Venice lasted more than 1,100 years. It was never a huge empire, but it controlled trade routes and kept its independence through wars and political upheaval that wiped out other states.

Even Ethiopia had an empire that lasted from the 1200s until 1974. It is one of the only African nations that avoided full colonization and kept its monarchy for centuries.

III. Why the Long-Lasting Empires Fell

Even the strongest empires eventually fall. Some collapse fast. Others fade over generations. But every one of them had weak points that grew over time. When enough of those piled up, the system could not hold together anymore.

The Roman Empire

Rome controlled most of Europe, North Africa, and the Middle East at its peak. But by the time the western half fell in 476, it was already in deep trouble. There were too many wars. The empire stretched too far and cost too much to defend. Corruption and bad leadership drained resources. The rich got richer, the poor got poorer, and the middle class vanished. Rome relied heavily on slave labor, so innovation slowed. As the empire weakened from the inside, outside groups like the Visigoths and Vandals attacked from the outside.

The Byzantine Empire lasted another 1,000 years but faced constant wars, religious conflicts, and power struggles. The Ottomans took over Constantinople in 1453, and that was the end.

The Ottoman Empire

The Ottomans held a massive region for centuries. By the 1800s, they were already being called the "sick man of Europe." Their downfall came from military decline, rising nationalism, internal infighting, and resistance to reform. When World War I hit, they backed the losing side. The war broke the empire, and modern-day Turkey took its place in 1922.

Ancient Egypt

Egypt lasted for thousands of years through different dynasties. Eventually, weak leadership and invasions by outsiders like the Assyrians and Persians wore it down. Alexander the Great took control in 332 BCE, and by 30 BCE, it became part of the Roman Empire.

The Republic of Venice

Venice relied on trade and diplomacy to stay powerful. But the rise of Atlantic trade routes left it behind. It also avoided major alliances and fell behind militarily. Napoleon conquered Venice in

1797 without much resistance.

The Ethiopian Empire

Ethiopia kept its monarchy for centuries. They resisted colonization longer than any other African country, though it was briefly occupied by Italy from 1936 to 1941. After that came internal unrest, famine, and a Marxist coup in 1974. The empire ended, replaced by dictatorship.

The Mongol Empire

The Mongols built the largest land empire ever. But after Genghis Khan died, his heirs fought over power. The empire split, and by 1368 it had mostly collapsed.

The Spanish Empire

Spain controlled much of the world but got rich too fast. The silver and gold from the Americas caused inflation. Wars drained resources. By the early 1800s, most colonies had broken away.

The Habsburg Empire

The Habsburgs ruled Central Europe for centuries. But they governed a mix of cultures and languages without sharing power. World War I finished what internal tension had already started. The empire collapsed in 1918.

The Song Dynasty

The Song era in China saw major innovation. But the dynasty paid off enemies instead of defending itself. The Mongols eventually overran it in 1279.

The Maurya Empire

India's Maurya Empire reached its height under Emperor Ashoka. After he died, weak rulers let it fall apart. It lasted just over a century.

The Khmer Empire

The Khmer Empire dominated much of what is now Cambodia and extended its influence into parts of modern-day Thailand, Laos, and Vietnam. They built cities like Angkor Wat. But drought, failed agriculture, and invasions ended their power by 1431.

Each of these empires was powerful in its time. Each lasted longer than the United States has so far. But they all fell for reasons that feel familiar: too much expansion, not enough reform, ignoring unrest, or falling behind in technology.

IV. What the U.S. Can Learn from the Collapse of Older Empires

History is full of warnings. Big, powerful nations rise and fall all the time. It rarely happens overnight. It happens when small cracks are ignored for too long. The United States still has time to avoid that fate, but only if it pays attention.

1. Do not stretch too far or spend too much

Rome, Spain, and the Mongols overreached. They spent on far-off wars while neglecting problems at home. The U.S. spends more on defense than the next ten countries combined. But schools and infrastructure are falling apart.

2. When the middle collapses, the rest follows

Rome and the Ottomans lost their middle class. The same is happening in the U.S. Wages are flat. Costs rise. Wealth is hoarded. That is a recipe for instability.

3. National unity matters, but so does flexibility

Austria-Hungary forced unity on unwilling groups and collapsed. Byzantium survived longer by adapting. The U.S. is divided by class, race, and politics. If it cannot find common ground, it will break from within.

4. Cultural decay is a symptom, not the cause

Rome did not fall because of moral failure. It fell because its institutions rotted. People gave up. That can happen anywhere. The signs are showing in the U.S. too.

5. Technology alone will not save you

The Song Dynasty was advanced but still fell. Technology is not a shield. It must be paired with good leadership and working systems.

6. Every empire thinks it is the exception

Rome. Egypt. The Ottomans. They all thought they would last forever. They did not. Believing you are immune is the first step toward decline.

History does not repeat exactly. But it follows patterns. The fall of a nation does not always come with a bang. Often, it comes slow, through ignored warnings and small failures that pile up.

V. Conclusion: Flexibility is Essential

The United States has done incredible things in a short time. But every powerful country before it thought it was too big to fail. Every one of them was wrong.

What makes a country last is not wealth or weapons. It is how it handles pressure. Whether it can adapt. Whether it can take care of its people and fix what is broken.

Long-lasting civilizations do not survive by accident. They last because they stay flexible. Because they know the difference between pride and purpose.

The U.S. is at a crossroads. It can learn from the past. Or it can ignore it and make the same mistakes. The choice is still ours. But time is running out.

If we want this country to last, we need to start acting like it.

"Too Big to Fail": A Repeating Illusion in World History

What Collapsing Superpowers Never See Coming

Throughout history, empires and superpowers have often believed that their fall would trigger worldwide collapse. Whether rooted in hubris, fear, or genuine global reliance, they imagined themselves as keystones holding civilization together.

And yet, time after time, these "immovable" giants fell and the world, though shaken, adapted. Power shifted. New systems emerged. History didn't end. It simply turned a page.

The Spanish Empire

In the 16th and 17th centuries, Spain ruled vast territories across the Americas, extracting wealth through conquest, enslavement, and resource exploitation. The empire's might was built on silver from the New World and the labor of those it subjugated. But cracks appeared early.

Naval defeats (notably the failure of the Armada in 1588), economic inflation, overreliance on colonial wealth, and rising independence movements eroded its power. By the 19th century,

Spain's colonies in Latin America had revolted, and the empire was reduced to a shadow of its former self.

Global trade didn't end. It simply flowed through new routes.

The Portuguese Empire

Portugal once commanded a vast maritime empire that covered Brazil to Africa, India, and Southeast Asia. It was a pioneer of oceanic exploration and global trade.

But as larger European powers like Britain and the Netherlands expanded, Portugal couldn't keep up militarily or economically. It was increasingly constrained by British influence, and internal stagnation weakened its institutions. Decolonization, especially in Africa, would complete its decline in the 20th century.

The seas kept churning. Trade continued but under new flags.

The Qing Dynasty

The Qing ruled over modern China, Mongolia, Taiwan, and more, controlling as much as 30% of global GDP in the early 1800s. It had a strong bureaucracy and command structure admired across Asia.

Yet internal corruption, peasant uprisings, ethnic unrest,

and humiliations at the hands of Western powers (such as the Opium Wars and Boxer Rebellion) weakened the dynasty. In 1911, the Qing fell and ended over two millennia of imperial rule.

What followed wasn't instant resurgence. China endured civil war, foreign invasion, authoritarian upheaval, and economic chaos. But after generations of struggle, it reemerged as a global power but under vastly different terms.

The Ottoman Empire

The Ottomans ruled the Middle East, North Africa, and parts of Europe for over 600 years. They offered relative stability, religious pluralism, and early innovations in healthcare and infrastructure.

But by the 19th century, the empire was dubbed "the sick man of Europe." Nationalist uprisings, military defeats, and Western encroachment weakened its grip. World War I delivered the final blow.

Though the empire collapsed in 1922, new nations emerged in its place, including the secular Republic of Turkey. The region entered a period of volatility, but it did not vanish into chaos.

Note: Any fair history of the Ottomans must also acknowledge the repression and mass violence against minority groups, including the Armenian, Greek, and Assyrian peoples.

The British Empire

By the late 1800s, Britain ruled up to a quarter of the planet. It dominated global trade, finance, and naval power. People said, "the sun never sets on the British Empire."

But empire came at a cost, both to Britain and the people it ruled. Two world wars bankrupted the nation. Anti-colonial revolutions spread across Asia and Africa. Partition, rebellion, and sometimes brutal suppression marked the empire's end.

Britain retained cultural and financial influence through the Commonwealth and global institutions, but it never regained its imperial status. The world moved on in many ways, more multipolar and independent.

The Soviet Union

The USSR rose from the ashes of tsarist Russia to become the world's second superpower. It industrialized rapidly, helped defeat Nazi Germany, and put the first man in space. But the cost was staggering: famines, purges, gulags, and a surveillance state.

By the 1980s, economic stagnation, suppressed nationalist tensions, and an arms race with the United States strained the system. Gorbachev's reforms, notably glasnost (openness) and perestroika (restructuring) unintentionally accelerated its unraveling.

In 1991, the Soviet Union dissolved into 15 independent republics. The Cold War ended. Western institutions expanded. Russia reemerged, but the world order shifted dramatically.

The United States (Today)

Since World War II, the U.S. has seen itself as the "leader of the free world", a democratic, military, and cultural hegemon.

But today, questions linger. Political polarization, debt, inequality, and global competition (from China, the EU, and others) challenge American dominance. Some argue the U.S. remains indispensable. Others wonder if its peak has passed.

Still, if America's influence declines, it won't be the end, just another transition. Global power may disperse rather than collapse. As history shows, the system adapts. The stage resets. And the story continues.

Common Threads in Empire Decline

Overconfidence: Many believed their dominance was eternal and ignoring warning signs until it was too late.

Economic Mismanagement: Whether through overreliance on resource wealth, command economies, or war spending, cracks often began in the economy.

Colonial or Ethnic Unrest: The ruled do not stay silent

forever.

External Rivals: No empire falls in a vacuum. Competitors wait and rise.

Conclusion: Size Isn't Immunity

Empires, like people, imagine themselves as permanent. The phrase "If we fall, we take everyone with us" is often a bluff. It's not prophecy. It's fear of irrelevance spoken aloud.

Yes, the collapse of great powers brings real disruption. But history tells us clearly: the world does not end. It shifts. And a new chapter begins.

The Next Uprising Will Clock In: How to Reclaim Power One Union at a Time

What if the real structural reform doesn't come from Congress or courts—but from a break room in Buffalo, or a sidewalk in Bessemer?

I. The Forgotten Weapon

Before corporate PACs, before gerrymandering software, before cable news turned Congress into a stage—there were unions.

Not as footnotes, but as counterweights.

For decades, organized labor served as one of the only institutions capable of holding capital in check. It lifted wages, expanded protections, and pressured lawmakers to deliver for workers across race, gender, and geography. It wasn't perfect. But it was power.

Then we let it go.

Or rather—systematically dismantled it. And for a while, it looked like labor's time had passed. But now, something's shifting.

Not from the top down. From the floor up.

II. What Labor Used to Do

In the mid-20th century, union membership in the U.S. hovered above 30% (BLS). Entire industries—auto, steel, rail, public education—ran on collective bargaining.

Unions didn't just negotiate contracts. They funded civil rights marches. They fought for workplace safety and unemployment insurance. They pulled children out of factories and pushed retirement into law.

They weren't passive policy followers. They were engines of structural change.

Today, only about 10% of U.S. workers belong to a union (BLS, 2023). But in sectors like retail and logistics—where the old model never took root—new movements are forming anyway.

The **National Labor Relations Act** (NLRA) is now nearly a century old. It's underfunded and toothless, letting employers fire organizers with trivial penalties while gig workers lack clear protections.

III. How It Was Undone

Labor didn't collapse by accident. It was targeted.

The **Taft-Hartley Act** (1947) restricted strikes and banned secondary boycotts. "Right-to-work" laws spread through the South and Midwest, undermining dues structures. In 1981, Ronald Reagan fired 11,000 striking air traffic controllers, opening the floodgates for corporate retaliation.

Then came outsourcing, gig classification, and the *Janus v. AFSCME* ruling, which weakened public unions by making dues optional.

Democrats chased donors instead of defending workers. Labor was sidelined by the same politicians who once called it the backbone of democracy.

IV. The New Labor Movement Doesn't Look Like the Old One

It's not coming from steel mills. It's coming from espresso counters, grocery stores, warehouses, and Genius Bars.

The new labor wave is younger, browner, more female—and Gen Z sees labor not as a throwback, but as a survival tool.

Starbucks baristas, led by Workers United, organized over 350 stores after a 2022 Twitter thread detailing brutal working conditions went viral with over 2 million views, sparking walkouts and GoFundMe mutual aid campaigns.

In Staten Island, Chris Smalls and the Amazon Labor Union built their campaign with clipboards, a grill, and a tent in the parking lot—rallied by a Reddit thread that mobilized over 10,000 online supporters.

Organizing is now digital-first. The strike lives on Discord. Solidarity spreads by meme. This is labor without permission.

V. Why Now?

The pandemic exposed the lie that hard work pays.

"Essential" workers got applause, not raises, while executives profited from vacation homes. Rent spiked. Inflation soared. The wealth gap widened.

Workers watched their lives shrink while companies bragged about record earnings. Loyalty didn't just erode. It collapsed—and was replaced by organizing.

VI. What's Still Blocking Them

Employers exploit a broken system. They fire organizers, delay elections, and hire law firms like Littler Mendelson to crush union drives—knowing the consequences are years away, if they ever arrive.

Captive-audience meetings. Surveillance. Blacklisting. Intimidation disguised as "coaching." These aren't outliers. They're strategy.

The law enables it. And the cost of pushing back often falls entirely on the workers.

VII. Counterarguments—And Why They Miss the Mark

Critics say unions are outdated, hurt businesses, or unwanted by younger workers.

But gig workers—like Uber drivers who went on strike in 10 cities in 2023—are organizing globally to fight algorithmic exploitation.

Sectoral bargaining gives small businesses a level playing field and helps raise wages while reducing turnover (EPI, 2022).

And Gen Z? They're the most pro-union generation alive (Gallup, 2022), with majority support across demographics and income brackets.

The future isn't anti-union. It's waiting for legal permission to build one.

VIII. What Real Reform Would Look Like

Reform starts with teeth. Then leverage. Then visibility.

- **Card Check**: Allow union formation with majority support—no election manipulation.

- **Repeal Taft-Hartley**: Restore the right to solidarity strikes and economic pressure.

- **Gig Worker Reclassification**: End the "independent contractor" loophole at the federal level.

- **Sectoral Bargaining**: Raise standards across industries instead of competing race-to-the-bottom shops.

- **Penalize Retaliation**: Mandatory reinstatement and major fines for illegal firings.

- **Union Incentives**: Prioritize federal contracts for unionized or neutrality-agreement employers.

Readers can amplify this wave by joining a local picket line, donating to the Amazon Labor Union's GoFundMe, or supporting the PRO Act via campaigns like ActBlue Labor.

IX. Why This Isn't Just About Wages

Yes, unions raise pay. But their real power is structural.

They increase civic participation. Build democratic capacity. Weaken authoritarian creep. In countries with strong unions, inequality is lower, social trust is higher, and institutional legitimacy lasts longer (OECD, 2020).

Unions don't just bargain for benefits. They negotiate who gets a voice.

X. Conclusion: The Strike Is a Signal

A picket line is more than a contract fight. It's a line drawn against a system that only listens when workers scream through closed fists or quit quietly.

This revival isn't nostalgic. It's adaptive. It's scrappy, leaderless, multilingual, and often anonymous. It's anti-permission.

If you want to track the future of political power in America, stop staring at the Senate floor.
Start watching the sidewalk outside your nearest Starbucks.

Who's Even in Charge Here?

How State and Federal Preemption Laws Suppress—and Sometimes Protect—Local Democracy

Across the country, a quiet power struggle is reshaping American democracy—not between parties, but between levels of government. Cities and counties, often the first to experiment with new policies, are increasingly finding their hands tied by state or federal laws designed to override local authority. This maneuver, called *preemption*, allows higher levels of government to block or nullify laws passed by local ones.

In theory, preemption ensures legal consistency across jurisdictions. But in practice, it is increasingly used as a tool of suppression—not coordination. Local governments trying to raise wages, pass environmental protections, or enact civil rights ordinances are routinely overruled by legislatures more responsive to donors than constituents.

This is federalism turned on its head: a structure designed to share power now used to consolidate it.

I. What Is Preemption?

Preemption comes in two primary forms:

- **Federal preemption** occurs when federal law overrides state or local law. This authority is rooted in the Constitution's Supremacy Clause.

- **State preemption** allows states to override local laws—especially in states that don't offer "home rule" protections to their cities.

Used responsibly, preemption can provide clarity, especially in areas like transportation systems or civil rights enforcement. But when it's deployed to serve donors and deter innovation, it becomes a mechanism of political control. And today, that's increasingly the case.

II. Local Innovation, State Veto

Local governments have long acted as laboratories of democracy—testing policies in response to local needs. But many of those innovations are short-lived, wiped out by preemption laws passed under pressure from well-funded interest groups.

- **Minimum Wage:** Birmingham, Alabama, passed a $10.10 minimum wage ordinance. The state legislature immediately banned all cities from setting their own wage floors. Similar laws now exist in over 25 states.

- **Housing and Zoning:** Cities like Boulder, Colorado, have passed rent control measures, only to be blocked by state-level bans. Arizona prohibits cities from restricting short-term rentals, even when local residents say they drive up housing costs.

- **Public Health:** During COVID-19, governors in Texas and Florida banned cities from enforcing mask mandates—even in areas with high transmission.

- **Environmental Protections:** Pennsylvania and Texas passed laws barring local restrictions on fracking. Plastic bag bans and pesticide regulations have also been overturned in multiple states.

- **Civil Rights:** North Carolina's HB2 law voided local LGBTQ+ protections. Tennessee prohibits municipalities from removing Confederate monuments, even with local support.

In each case, preemption was used not to resolve conflict—but to suppress policy differences that reflected local priorities.

III. Preemption Defended—and Distorted

Supporters of preemption often argue it prevents chaos: that it avoids a confusing patchwork of laws, reduces compliance costs, and preserves state sovereignty.

Those arguments hold water in narrow cases. Some businesses, particularly smaller firms, worry that differing local ordinances create unpredictable compliance costs. And in fields like environmental safety, unified standards can prevent regulatory gaps.

But these concerns are often overstated—and opportunistically framed by corporate lobbying groups like ALEC. Wage preemption bills, for instance, are almost never championed by small businesses; they're written by national industry associations prioritizing profit over workers. And when preemption blocks a city from banning dangerous pesticides near schools, it's hard to argue the real motive is efficiency.

Preemption can protect against chaos—but it can just as easily enforce uniform stagnation.

IV. Who Benefits—and Who Fights Back

Preemption doesn't happen in a vacuum. It's driven by organized power.

- **ALEC** (the American Legislative Exchange Council) crafts boilerplate legislation to block local ordinances—from minimum wage hikes to paid sick leave—then disseminates those bills through state legislatures.

- **Think tanks and industry coalitions** back those efforts with research, legal support, and PR campaigns. Cities are painted as reckless or radical. Lawsuits follow.

- **Political consultants and party leaders** push talking points that portray local governments as unserious or overreaching—even when they're responding directly to constituents.

When Austin tried to mandate paid sick leave, corporate lobbies filed lawsuits and the Texas Legislature passed a preemption law to strike it down statewide. Similar tactics followed efforts to regulate plastic bags, control short-term rentals, and expand anti-discrimination protections.

Still, resistance works. In 2018, Michigan voters passed a redistricting reform ballot initiative after lawmakers blocked similar local efforts. In Missouri, Kansas City residents fought back against police preemption with public campaigns that drew national attention.

Preemption thrives in the dark. When it's exposed, it can be challenged.

V. When Preemption Protects

Not all preemption is regressive. At its best, it protects rights and ensures basic standards.

- **Federal civil rights laws** override discriminatory state and local rules.
- **The Voting Rights Act** once preempted racially motivated

election laws—until gutted by *Shelby County v. Holder.*

- **Environmental standards** like the **Clean Air Act** prevent dangerous gaps in protections.

International examples show how to draw this line more intentionally.

In **Germany**, the constitutional principle of *subsidiarity* ensures decisions are made at the lowest level unless a clear national interest justifies otherwise. Courts enforce this balance.

In **Canada**, charter cities like **Toronto** negotiate formal agreements with provinces, giving them greater autonomy in specific domains like transit, land use, or public health. These agreements protect local control while allowing for coordination.

In the U.S., no such structural safeguard exists. Preemption is assumed valid unless challenged, giving higher governments a blank check to erase local decisions.

VI. What Reform Could Look Like

1. Expand Home Rule:

Enshrine local autonomy in state constitutions. This would protect cities from arbitrary overrides.

> *Trade-off:* Local policies could diverge significantly, complicating state-level coordination. Germany mitigates this through constitutional review and judicial standards—balancing flexibility with clarity.

2. Judicial Standards for Review:

Courts should evaluate preemption laws based on public interest, not just jurisdictional hierarchy.

> *Trade-off:* Critics may claim this invites judicial overreach. But transparent legal criteria, applied consistently, can help build legitimacy.

3. Require Impact Assessments:

Preemption bills should include reports on their likely effects—on wages, housing, civil rights, or the environment—before being passed.

4. Invest in Public Education:

Broad-based campaigns can raise awareness of how preemption affects daily life.

> Example: **FairVote's** educational work on electoral reform helped normalize complex topics. Similar strategies could build public understanding of how preemption blocks action on wages, rent, and rights.

5. Empower Ballot Initiatives:

Where possible, use direct democracy to override legislative suppression. Michigan's 2018 redistricting campaign succeeded despite establishment resistance.

6. Charter Agreements for Cities:

Like Toronto, U.S. cities could negotiate formal agreements with their states to protect specific policy domains—housing, policing, or health—from preemption.

Each reform strengthens democratic structure—restoring local agency while preserving space for coordinated standards.

VII. Conclusion: Local Power Is Real Power—If We Protect It

Preemption can be a legitimate tool. But more often, it's used to erase the voices of local communities in service of centralized agendas. It substitutes uniformity for consent and turns shared governance into a game of top-down control.

A healthy federalism requires more than tiers of government. It requires shared purpose—and clear boundaries.

If we want to protect the places where reform most often begins—cities, counties, and neighborhoods—we have to defend their right to govern. That means:

- Supporting home rule amendments in your state.
- Joining organizations like the **Local Solutions Support Center** that fight preemption abuses.
- Calling out when state or federal officials silence local voices—not for the sake of order, but for the sake of power.

Because democracy isn't just something we vote for at the top.

It's something we build from the bottom up.

Epilogue: If You're Reading This, Things Went to Hell

Ten legal, disciplined, mass-scale steps to force change in a system that's clearly collapsed, serves no one, and somehow still expects us to pay bills, answer emails, and pretend voting matters. Everything's broken. No one's steering. So, sure—I'll ride to D.C. with you. What are they gonna do, collapse harder?

This is not a call to violence. This is not a fantasy. It is a scenario—a thought experiment grounded in law, nonviolence, and logistics. It is intended only for a moment when every reform effort has failed, and even the illusion of representation has worn thin. If you're reading this in that moment, the following is the last tool left that does not rely on force, money, or permission alone.

I. Stop Asking

Power does not concede because it is asked. If you've marched, called, voted, petitioned, organized, and the system still grinds on untouched, then it is no longer confused. It is insulated. Stop appealing to institutions that have structurally locked you out. They do not ask for belief, only recognition—that legitimacy requires consent, and consent can be withdrawn.

II. Break Routine

What those in power fear is not chaos. It is interruption. Systems built on ceremony and order cannot withstand lawful disruption at scale. You do not need violence to stop a machine. You only need to wedge something solid into its gears. Interrupting ritual is more dangerous to power than rage. When the chamber can't convene and the cameras can't cut away, the machine begins to stall.

III. Show Up

If 100,000 unarmed citizens calmly surrounded the Capitol and refused to leave, nothing could continue as normal. No demands. No slogans. Just presence. A visible, lawful, immovable audit of legitimacy. Not chaos. Not threat. Just a refusal to go away.

IV. Authorities Respond—And Logistics Respond Faster

Authorities cut water to parks. Bathrooms are locked. Trash collection halts. Curfews are declared. But the crowd is ready. Large donors fund mobile sanitation, clean water tanks, and food service from the 300+ food trucks in D.C. Portable toilets are cleaned on schedule. Water is distributed by volunteer crews. Nothing collapses. Everything adapts.

V. Food Keeps Coming

Feeding 100,000 people isn't easy. But it happens—not through one funder, but hundreds. The lines stay orderly. Meals rotate by zone. One food truck plays Marvin Gaye. Another hands out apples wrapped in copies of the First Amendment. The trucks never stop. The crowds stay fed. The Capitol cafeteria? Not so much. The cafeteria breaks open the reserves. Someone inside the Senate House doesn't get their normal lunch and is slightly irritated. Someone outside is eating a sandwich that they will remember for decades.

VI. The City Doesn't Burn. It Gridlocks.

The protest zone is quiet. Medics move freely. Livestreamers document every moment. Tourists start arriving just to witness it. No flags. No fights. Just pressure. Just too many people for a city to function normally.

VII. Police Hesitate

No broken windows. No provocations. The optics of force are too risky. Officers refuse orders. Some quietly defect. A few bring supplies.

VIII. The National Guard Arrives. Then Idles.

What do you do with 100,000 seated, sunburned Americans handing out sandwiches and reciting constitutional amendments on camera? You don't fire tear gas into a crowd with six angles of livestream. You don't arrest grandmothers next to veterans reading the Bill of Rights. Not unless you want the whole world to see what side you're on.

IX. Support Doesn't Always Look Like Cheering

Protest isn't always shouting. It's standing back. It's the shop owner who lets medics use the restroom. It's the bus driver who doesn't stop for blockades. It's the landlord who doesn't evict a protester. It's the citizens who let protesters sleep in shifts in their backyards. Passive solidarity holds the line.

X. And Inside the Building, Someone Blinks

A lawmaker walks out. Another tweets a message of support. A third gives a floor speech that's piped through portable speakers to the outside. The dam doesn't break—but it starts to leak.

Logistics Make It Real

Water: 100,000 gallons per day is a challenge—but not a barrier. With planning, mobile tanks, and refill stations, it's covered. Toilets: ~1,300 portable units, cleaned on rotation, keeps the site humane. Food: Local trucks, donor funding, mutual aid. Real logistics, real money, real outcomes. Medical: Volunteer paramedics, mobile clinics, and soft support from sympathetic providers.

Water trucks refill daily from regional facilities outside the protest zone. Portable refill stations are spaced throughout the crowd grid. Hydration crews patrol on foot with rolling coolers and refill jugs. Shade tents and mist stations provide relief. Heat stroke protocols are rehearsed like drills. There are no second chances in summer.

Sanitation is handled with discipline. Pump trucks must access each portable toilet on a fixed cleaning schedule. Volunteer marshals keep clear routes open for service vehicles. Each restroom block is tagged and mapped. Waste is transported offsite daily through contracted haulers funded by pooled donations. Hygiene crews monitor conditions closely—because if morale breaks, so does the occupation.

Trash doesn't pile up. Volunteers sweep assigned zones in rolling shifts every eight hours. Contractor bags are bundled and staged for pickup. Makeshift drop points are created for recycling. Each lane is someone's job. The crowd holds the line, and the line stays clean.

Feeding 100,000 people isn't cheap. It might take $4–5

million to keep 100 trucks going for a month—but it happens. Not through one funder, but hundreds. QR codes appear on cardboard signs. Spreadsheet links circulate. Union locals sponsor full-day shifts. Teachers Venmo $10 from kitchen tables. The crowds stay fed through community support, while helicopters deliver crates of supplies overhead—to Congress. The contrast is impossible to miss: aid from the sky for those inside the building, while the people outside feed each other.

Sleeping shifts rotate in layers. Some protesters stay overnight in tents or cars. Others return during the day and go home to rest. A few rent Airbnbs or crash with relatives in nearby neighborhoods. Some are billeted by locals—retirees, students, even civil servants who want to help but can't be seen on camera. Portable showers are set up in controlled areas. Handwashing stations and sanitation tents are supplied with donated soap, menstrual kits, and hygiene gear.

The question isn't whether people would come. It's how you get enough of them to come at the same time—and how you keep them there.

History offers more guidance than it gets credit for. In 2025, over a million people showed up to see Lady Gaga on Copacabana Beach. Not for a protest. Not for survival. Just for music. That same location has hosted crowd sizes over two million for New Year's Eve.

The key isn't mass belief—it's mass attention. You don't need a viral petition or a charismatic leader. You need a dozen people everyone already recognizes—not to headline, not to give speeches, but to quietly show up. Sit on the lawn. Walk with the crowd. Maybe pick up a drum. Their job isn't to entertain. It's to normalize participation.

They aren't there for a show. They're there for the same reason everyone else is: because enough is enough. That makes them unspinnable.

Think less MLK at the podium, more Bruce Springsteen crossing the National Mall with a thermos. Think Rage Against the Machine just being there. Think Dolly Parton or Weird Al holding a sign, not a mic. Imagine Eddie Vedder or Killer Mike explaining the constitution to young people. Think anyone who draws a cross-generational crowd and doesn't back down from a moment of truth.

And then think about what not to do. Look at Woodstock '99. Look at Altamont. Look at the unprepared infrastructure, the overpriced water, the lack of safety protocols. Any mass assembly that treats logistics as an afterthought will devolve—into chaos, into violence, or into a PR disaster. The same goes for messaging. No stage-rants. No soapboxes. No party endorsements.

Just people. Together. Not angry. Not screaming. Not even

blocking roads. Just standing—calm, massive, immovable.

That's the image that can't be spun. That's the image that lives in the world's memory. And it doesn't take all of us. Just enough to not be ignored.

Final Thought

This isn't symbolism.
It's not protest culture.
It's a pressure tactic.

No speeches. No slogans. No violence.
Just 100,000 people refusing to leave.

Not a riot. Not a threat.
Just a presence so sustained, so disciplined, and so massive that the system starts asking itself how long it can hold.

Because it's not force that drives change.
It's **the implication**—
the unspoken awareness that if this many people are willing to come this far without breaking,
they might not stop when asked.
They might not stay polite.
And they absolutely won't go home empty-handed.

If it works, there won't be fireworks.

There will be concessions.

There will be silence.

There will be fear.

And then—there will be movement.

Sources

Broockman, D. E., & Skovron, C. (2022). *Bias in Perceptions of Public Opinion Among Political Elites*. American Pol. Sci. Review.

Brown v. Board of Education, 347 U.S. 483 (1954).

Citizens United v. Federal Election Commission, 558 U.S. 310 (2010).

Dobbs v. Jackson Women's Health Organization, 597 U.S. ___ (2022).

Fairbank, J. K. (2006). *China: A New History* (2nd ed.). Harvard University Press.

Ferguson, N. (2003). *Empire: The Rise and Demise of the British World Order*. Basic Books.

Gallup. (2022). *Trust in government and democratic institutions* [Survey].

Germany. (2018). *Network Enforcement Act (NetzDG)*.

History.com Editors. (n.d.). Why Rome fell. *History.com*. Retrieved from https://www.history.com

Kinross, L. (1977). *The Ottoman Centuries: The Rise and Fall of the Turkish Empire*. William Morrow.

Levitsky, S., & Ziblatt, D. (2018). *How Democracies Die*.

Crown Publishing.

Maine Secretary of State. (n.d.). *Ranked-choice voting implementation.*

McCain-Feingold Act, Bipartisan Campaign Reform Act of 2002, Pub. L. No. 107-155, 116 Stat. 81.

Michigan Independent Citizens Redistricting Commission. (n.d.). *Commission history and structure.*

Moore v. Harper, 600 U.S. ___ (2023).

National Public Radio. (n.d.). *Title 42 expulsions and immigration policy.*

New York City Civic Engagement Commission. (n.d.). *Participatory budgeting overview.*

OpenSecrets.org. (2023). *Federal campaign finance and donor data.*

Parker, G. (1999). *The Spanish Empire: A Historical Encyclopedia.* ABC-CLIO.

Patriot Act, Uniting and Strengthening America by Providing Appropriate Tools Required to Intercept and Obstruct Terrorism Act of 2001, Pub. L. No. 107-56, 115 Stat. 272.

Pew Research Center. (2023). *Democracy and constitutional trust surveys.*

Reform Party. (n.d.). *History and electoral participation.*

Roe v. Wade, 410 U.S. 113 (1973).

Seattle Ethics and Elections Commission. (n.d.). *Democracy Vouchers Program.*

Shelby County v. Holder, 570 U.S. 529 (2013).

South African Government. (1996). *Constitution of the Republic of South Africa.*

Swedish Election Authority. (n.d.). *Voter turnout and registration policies.*

Taubman, W. (2017). *Gorbachev: His Life and Times.* Simon & Schuster.

Tillman Act, Act of Jan. 26, 1907, ch. 420, 34 Stat. 864.

Tunisia National Dialogue Quartet. (2011). *Labor-led political transition.*

U.S. Congress. (2002). *Bipartisan Campaign Reform Act.*

U.S. Supreme Court. *Burwell v. Hobby Lobby Stores, Inc.*, 573 U.S. 682 (2014).

Wallace, G. (1968). *American Independent Party campaign archives.*

Ziblatt, D., & Levitsky, S. (2018). *How Democracies Die.* Crown Publishing.

About the Author

James "JiLm" Ergle is a political essayist, cartoonist, and criminal investigator. By day, he digs through sealed court records and broken systems. By night, he explains how they work—and how to dismantle them. He writes for people who know something's wrong but want more than slogans. He writes regularly at Radical Leanings, where essays and political cartoons cut through media noise to trace the roots of dysfunction. (By the way, the L is silent.)

www.ingramcontent.com/pod-product-compliance
Lightning Source LLC
Chambersburg PA
CBHW020534030426
42337CB00013B/845